inevitable

RELATIONSHIP SUCCESS

Where Marriage, Parenting, and Ministry Thrive

SHANNON O'DELL

WESTBOW
PRESS®
A DIVISION OF THOMAS NELSON
& ZONDERVAN

Scripture taken from the Holy Bible, NEW INTERNATIONAL VERSION®. Copyright © 1973, 1978, 1984, 2011 by Biblica, Inc. All rights reserved worldwide. Used by permission. NEW INTERNATIONAL VERSION® and NIV® are registered trademarks of Biblica, Inc. Use of either trademark for the offering of goods or services requires the prior written consent of Biblica US, Inc.

WestBow Press books may be ordered through booksellers or by contacting:

WestBow Press
A Division of Thomas Nelson & Zondervan
1663 Liberty Drive
Bloomington, IN 47403
www.westbowpress.com
1 (866) 928-1240

ISBN: 978-1-5127-4937-3(sc)
ISBN: 978-1-5127-4938-0 (hc)
ISBN: 978-1-5127-4936-6 (e)

Library of Congress Control Number: 2016911546

Print information available on the last page.

WestBow Press rev. date: 08/08/2016

ACKNOWLEDGEMENTS

To Jesus – thank you for the invitation to eat at your table March 15, 1981.

To my gorgeous wife Cindy – you make this book possible. Thank you for making our table a family priority, and so welcoming to those seeking a relationship with Christ.

To my kids – Anna, Evan, Sara, and KJ. Family table moments are some of my most treasured memories. You have an INEVITABLE future filled with relationship success.

To my church – thank you Brand New Church for making it so much fun to serve God.

To my mentor and pastor – Pastor Ed Young Jr. for sparking this truth in my heart. Thank you for shaping my life, marriage, and ministry.

To Tim Dudley and Todd Hillard – thank you for making this project possible.

To Martha Plumlee – Who invited me to her table so I could have an inevitable relationship with Jesus Christ.

WHAT OTHER LEADERS ARE SAYING

In his book, *Inevitable*, Shannon O'Dell uniquely speaks in a language that connects with his readers and assuring a pathway to success in life's most driving passions. With candor Shannon gives insightful and practical steps for health in marriage, family, and ministry. Read the book. Be challenged. And be greatly helped.
Dr. Claude Thomas, President
C3Global
Grapevine, Texas

Shannon O'Dell's book, *Inevitable*, brings new meaning to the significance of the Table in our lives. Discover the four legs of the table (one being sex) and how to keep the table upright. Don't allow the table to turn, use the tips he offers to help you keep your marriage rock solid and red-hot!
David Crank, Senior Pastor/Founder
FaithChurch.com
St. Louis, MO and West Palm Beach, FL

"When I was growing up, my parents had one major rule that was not easily relaxed, negotiated or changed. That rule was that every day at dinnertime we would all come to the table. In a similar way, this book guides all of us towards a consistent pattern of relational "table time" and "table talk". I'm excited about the inevitable breakthroughs and progress the truths of this book will bring to relationships."
Kevin Gerald, Lead Pastor
Champions Centre
Tacoma and Bellevue, WA

Shannon O'Dell keeps it real and tells it raw all the while making it reachable in his book on life, family and marriage. Moving away from relational ideology and rhetoric he pours his own life out empowering each reader with the confidence that this is not just a "how to" but a "can do" book. As you read this book prepare for authenticity and accuracy on how best to have relationships from a biblical point of view.

Marty Sloan, Lead Pastor
Harvest Time Church
Fort Smith, AR

In our fast-paced, drive-thru society, we have quickly lost the art form of a sit-down meal. Sadly, we rush through our food and fly over conversation. Yet, it is often at the table where everything can change… and it's not just in the dining room.

In his latest book, *INEVITABLE,* my good friend Shannon O'Dell sits us down and reminds us of the power of the table. By setting a place for us at various tables in the Bible, Shannon awakens readers to the potential and power the table can have in ministry, relationships, and life. Before you sit down for another meal, you need to read this book!

Ed Young
Pastor, Fellowship Church
Grapevine, TX
Author, You! The Journey to the Center of Your Worth

I've been watching Shannon lead his family and love his wife for more than two decades. What he writes here exemplifies what he's practiced—but even more…it is pure gold. Every couple who cares about their marriage, or wants to save it, should read this book.

Tim Stevens
Vanderbloemen Search Group
Author, Fairness is Overrated

Shannon O'Dell's *"Inevitable"* explores the art of intentional living, and how we can follow the example Christ set for us in the Word. Written from a fresh, real, and raw perspective, Inevitable gives practical and

biblical insight on how to build our lives upon the practice of gathering and engaging around the table. This book is a must-read for anyone interested in moving beyond just "letting life happen", and instead choosing a life of purpose - with a message that is challenging, thought provoking, and sure to inspire a new life in your marriage, needed encouragement as you parent, and fresh inspiration in your ministry.
Galen Woodward
Pastor, Copper Pointe Church
Albuquerque, NM
Author, Changing Church

My friend Shannon has done it again! He has gone written another GAME CHANGING book. As a gifted writer Shannon shares with every reader through personal experiences, humor, and spot on biblical teaching tools needed to see MARRIAGES GROW STRONGER, MARRIAGES RESTORED, and what GODS PLAN for MARRIAGE LOOKS LIKE! Its INEVITABLE that our lives and our marriages will be greatly impacted by this book and will IMPACT GENERATIONS TO COME! This is a must read, an incredible resource for every church, every small group, every marriage and every relationship!
Anthony Milas
Pastor, Granite United Church
Salem, NH

Shannon O'Dell is one of the most interesting church leaders in America that God is raising up to help His church flourish in today's world. One of the reasons for this is Shannon's ability to speak into the lives of people right where they are living, without ever compromising the Truth of God's Word. His newest book on marriage, love and romance will move you forward in your life and marriage.
Dr. Ronnie Floyd
President, Southern Baptist Convention
Senior Pastor, Cross Church
Springdale, AR

Shannon O'Dell has written *Inevitable* with refreshing vulnerability. Using the simple image of a table, and examples from his real life experiences, he's placed practical tools on every page to build a better marriage.
Steven Furtick
Pastor, Elevation Church
New York Times Best-selling Author
Charlotte, NC

"*Inevitable...* is a relationship success manual that even dudes will enjoy! Whether beginning, repairing or enhancing your marriage, Inevitable offers the practical wisdom, biblical insights, hilarious honesty and real answers that can move your relationship forward."
Scott Thomas
Lead Pastor, Free Life Chapel
Lakeland, FL

CONTENTS

INTRODUCTION

A Knock at the Door

table [t+ey-b*uh* l] *noun.*
1. An article of furniture consisting of a flat, slab-like top supported on one or more legs or other supports.
2. One of the most powerful, strategic tools ever given to us by God to build fantastic, eternally significant relationships.

Four and a half years ago, I had never seen a table before. Oh sure, I *saw* them everywhere, just like you do: Flat-topped, legs of differing length, usually with chairs or benches for sitting. Yeah, you see tables everywhere all the time—so often that I bet you don't even think about them. If you are like me, you have taken tables for granite. After all these years, I have to admit; I had never really *seen* tables for what they really are.

Then, one day, God flipped a switch in my head, the lights came on, and WHAM! Now, I'll never look at a table the same again. My mentor, and friend, Pastor Ed Young Jr. taught a leadership metaphor that the church was like a table. After that moment all relationships were viewed as tables, and all relationships are more effective at the table.

Tables aren't about furniture, they are about *relationships*—and they always have been.

I know, tables are designed for setting stuff *on* them. But what really matters is who is sitting *at* them. They might be covered with food or books or tools or coffee cups or bylaws or budgets, but when two or more people are seated around a table? Stuff can happen—*important stuff*—the kind of stuff that can ignite one person to change the world or change the world for one person. *That's* what tables are about. "At the table" is where marriage, parenting and ministry thrive... or die.

Seriously, stop for moment and think about some of the most wonderful, picturesque relational moments of communion that you have had with the people that you love the most. Think about the commitment, relational depth, moments of intimacy, moments where you heard some of the most endearing conversation and communication from your children. Think about contracts that were signed, decisions that were made, proposals that were laid out... this is the stuff that happens at the table. It's a place where every relationship in our life can be measured and nurtured... or destroyed.

It doesn't matter what a table is made of or where it might be. What matters is what happens when you are sitting or serving at one.

When I look back at all the amazing stuff that has happened to me at tables, I'm pretty much blown away. I was at a neighbor's dining room table when the wife invited my family to her church (a simple invitation that changed the direction of our whole family). I was at a table when my mom explained to me about the rapture and hell (a simple explanation that changed the direction my eternity). I was at a table when I fell in love with my wife, Cindy, and at a different table when I asked her to marry me. Our first argument was around a ping-pong table (I beat her and she was not accustomed to losing). After twenty some years of marriage, she and I have sat at tables uncountable times—praying, thinking, arguing, and making decisions that really matter. As we navigate our way through the good times and the harsh times, we connect at the tables in our home, restaurants and coffee shops.

And then I think about my family. As our family grew, so did our tables. Highchairs and booster seats and spilled milk. Yeah, the tables in our lives took some abuse during those years as we learned to love, and give, and discipline and talk in new ways. (And then there's always that trick of trying to scrape crusty Rice Crispies off the table with a belt sander, as the boys chew their graham crackers into the shape of a gun.

Throughout the book we will look at many of the amazing encounters Christ has with people at the table.

- He was Angered at Unjust Tables
  Matthew 21:12 "He overturned the tables of the money changers"

- He wanted the Needy served at The Table
  Acts 6:2 "It would not be right for us to neglect the ministry of the word of God in order to wait on tables."

- Judas betrayed Jesus at the Table
  Matthew 26:23 "Jesus replied, "The one who has dipped his hand into the bowl with me will betray me.

- Jesus reclined at the Table
  Matthew 26:20 "When evening came, Jesus was reclining at the table with the Twelve."

- After the Ascension went to the Table
  John 21:12 "Jesus said to them, "Come and have breakfast."

- Jesus first miracle was at the Table
  John 2:3 "When the wine was gone, Jesus' mother said to him, "They have no more wine."

- Jesus shared the Gospel at the Table
  Matthew 9:10 "While Jesus was having dinner at Matthew's house, many tax collectors and sinners came and ate with him and his disciples."

- Jesus taught miracles at the Table

Mark 6:39-41 "Then Jesus directed them to have all the people sit down in groups on the green grass. So they sat down in groups of hundreds and fifties. Taking the five loaves and the two fish and looking up to heaven, he gave thanks and broke the loaves"

- Jesus met with the Pharisee at the Table
  Luke 7:36 "When one of the Pharisees invited Jesus to have dinner with him, he went to the Pharisee's house and reclined at the table."

- Jesus declared His death at the Table
  Luke 22:19 "And he took bread, gave thanks and broke it, and gave it to them, saying, "This is my body given for you; do this in remembrance of me."

- Jesus after his ascension again went to the Table
  Luke 24:30 "When he was at the table with them, he took bread, gave thanks, broke it and began to give it to them."

- Heaven is at the Table
  Revelation 19:9 "Blessed are those who are invited to the wedding supper of the Lamb!"

You can see, Jesus was passionate about the table...and that is why we should be and why I felt is was important enough to write a book about it. What about these tables moments in the scripture...

- God's House had a Table
  1 Chronicles 28:16 "the weight of gold for each table for consecrated bread"

- God was betrayed at the Table
  Genesis 3:6 "When the woman saw that the fruit of the tree was good for food and pleasing to the eye, and also desirable for

gaining wisdom, she took some and ate it. She also gave some to her husband, who was with her, and he ate it."

- Cain betrayed his brother at the Offering Table
  Genesis 4:4 "And Abel also brought an offering—fat portions from some of the firstborn of his flock. The Lord looked with favor on Abel and his offering, 5 but on Cain and his offering he did not look with favor."

  Genesis 25: 33-34 "But Jacob said, "Swear to me first." So he swore an oath to him, selling his birthright to Jacob. Then Jacob gave Esau some bread and some lentil stew. He ate and drank, and then got up and left."

  Genesis 27:14 "So he went and got them and brought them to his mother, and she prepared some tasty food, just the way his father liked it."

- Joseph forgave his brothers at the Table
  Genesis 43:31 "After he had washed his face, he came out and, controlling himself, said, "Serve the food.""

- Esther declared her adversary at the Table
  Esther 7:1 "So the king and Haman went to Queen Esther's banquet"

As we take a closer look at some of those tables in the pages ahead you'll begin to see them in a different way, just like I do now. Most importantly, you'll see how the tables around you can be used for God's purposes in your marriage, family and ministry.

Yeah, the tables around me might look the same, but I sure don't see them the same anymore. The tables haven't changed, but the tables have definitely turned. The Bible can do that to you.

I love the story that a table can tell, and this book, *INEVITABLE*, is going to tell a lot of great stories and help you write some stories of your own. We are going to look at tables from the beginning of time till the end of time, recognizing God's Word really is a story that is found and told at a table. It starts when sin entered the world over a piece of fruit. It ends with a new beginning when, on Jesus' return, we will be as his bride seated at the wedding feast of the spotless, perfect, flawless Lamb of God. You and I, as Christ followers, will be seated at a table as we participate in eternity.

I pray that this will be a handbook for anyone who wants to know what a successful relationship looks like and feels like.

AT THE TABLE WITH JESUS

At the end of every chapter, you will be given an opportunity to respond to Christ's invitation to "eat with him". So 12 times I'm going to encourage you to try something is a little out of the box and take that invitation literally by sharing a meal or a dessert or a cup of coffee or something alone with Jesus. He promises that he will always be with you and promises that if you hear that knock on your door and opened it up, his spirit will actually come and live inside your spirit. You can do this at home at the kitchen counter or the dining room table. Or make it a picnic at the park or a water and snack break on a hike. You can even do it in a restaurant. (When the host seats you, ask for a table for two and two glasses of water, because you expecting that you'll be meeting with someone very important!)

I'm serious about this because belief filled with practical "how-to's" for earthly relationships create awesome stuff. But it's nothing compared to what is waiting for you at the table if you respond to the invitation Christ. When you do at the table? Keep it simple.

1. Ponder his words.
2. Share your heart with him.
3. Listen for him to share his heart with you through his Word and his Spirit.

AT THE TABLE WITH YOUR SPOUSE AND FAMILY

At the end of every chapter, I'll throw out some suggestions on how you can take the meat of each chapter, and serve it up as nourishment for deeper relationships with those who are closest to you. That might be your spouse, your family, or a small group that gets pulled together for the purpose of sharing what's happening at the table.

Tables can be strategically used to for protecting, nurturing and thriving in your marriage.

Table can be places where families interact like nowhere else. But do they? Do *we*? In many ways, the table of American family life is being threatened by cell phones and televisions and fast food and carpools and overflowing schedules. Those precious minutes of family interaction at the table are being lost. The scene where the Walton's and Cleaver's gathered at the end of each day are few and far between in this hectic age. And that's too bad. We are going to talk about reversing that trend, reclaiming the table for the family, and how to use tables all over the place to connect with your kids.

God has created you to love, worship and creatively build community. It doesn't matter where you are in life. The timeless principles of the table are drawn from God's Word and apply to singles, divorced, married and widowed young and old. If you have a heartbeat, this will light you up.

God has created marriage, family and ministry to be "tables" where we can serve the bread of life, Jesus, to others.

Trust me; this will make more sense as you begin to experience it in the chapters ahead as we investigate the "tables" of marriage, family and all relationships. You'll see that each of these relational "tables" is supported by four "legs"—vital values like communication, glory, honor training, creativity, wisdom and communication that keep each table standing. Most important is the leg of love, without which every table would be quickly topple.

When it starts to click, you will be amazed and empowered by a new facet of faith and relationships that God can use to start a groundswell of revival in your marriage, family and ministry. By dining at the table with Christ, and letting him nourish you as the eternal bread of life, you will be equipped to serve and invite others to feast at the table as well.

In this insane world, most of us are just trying to survive. But there really is a place where marriages, families and ministry can actually thrive.

It happened at the table in the Bible
It happens at the table today.
It will happen at the table in eternity…it's INEVITABLE.

THE MOST NOTABLE TABLE

From the beginning of His ministry at the wedding feast, at the last supper, to the fish dinner on the beach before the ascension and the wedding feast at His return, Jesus demonstrated the power of the table. Throughout this book we will look at some of the amazing encounters Christ had with people at the table. This is the real stuff. It's where allusions were shattered, truth was revealed, and people's hearts were changed for eternity. I call them "table moments" and all of them are important. Yet one table supersedes them all, and Christ himself invites us to that table in the Book of Revelation.

> Here I am! I stand at the door and knock. If anyone hears my voice and opens the door, I will come in and eat with that person, and they with me.
>
> —Revelation 3:20

This invitation was given to a specific church that really existed. The ancient ruins of Laodicea still stand today. It is an amazing place, made famous by its mineral hot springs that flow from the mountains. This was a popular place where the wealthy went for healing and, often, to die. Hot water was cherished and cool water was rare for refreshment. It was the lukewarm water flowing everywhere that had no real purpose… Just like so many people today who have no commitment or conviction as they go with the flow of the world. The invitation that Christ gave to them he gives to us too—an invitation to those who are floundering in the lukewarm stream of humanity.

What's the invitation? To open the door of our life and let Christ come in so you can eat with him. Yes, the table is powerful for marriage, family and ministry, but we are nothing but" lukewarm" until we have opened our hearts to him, and take full advantage of his invitation to sit across the table from him and eat together. Christ is calling you to the table--to his table—to an intimate, passionate relationship with him that supersedes all else.

This is what it's all about. It's a knock at the door, inviting you to dine at the table with Christ, the son of God, in person. It is a holy invitation. And make no mistake, it's not all dessert. There will be plenty of meat and potatoes and things that you probably won't want to swallow. Jesus rebukes and disciplines those he loves, so you can count on him leading you out of your comfort zones. Encounters with Jesus don't result in some sort tweak or adjustment. His Spirit and his Word are transformational, renewing your mind so you can do his will.

Exciting? No doubt. Scary? It should be. Just ask the guy with the coolest name in the entire Bible, Mephibosheth.

DEAD DOGS AT THE KING'S TABLE

Back in the day, new kings had a little tradition they followed with their old rivals: They killed them. In 1000 BC, a new king named David had killed a lot of them. It seemed like everybody was at war with everybody. The Philistines had trampled the armies of King Saul and his son Jonathan. David, a mighty warlord, was also an enemy of Saul, even though he was a close friend of Jonathan. When Saul and Jonathan were killed by Philistines, everyone assumed that David would rush into Saul's territory and kill what was left of Saul's family.

> Jonathan son of Saul had a son who was lame in both feet. He was five years old when the news about Saul and Jonathan came from Jezreel. His nurse picked him up and fled, but as she hurried to leave, he fell and became disabled. His name was Mephibosheth.—2 Samuel 4:4

Mephibosheth's name actually means, "Big Shame". In the Old Testament times, if you were crippled you were cursed. There were no two ways about it. If you were crippled you were seen as accursed and God had done the cursing. It was a shame that Mephibosheth was dropped and was crippled. It was a shame that he had to live in exile. It was a shame that he had to live with the guilt and the fear of being afraid of David. It was a shame that he was sold a pack of lies about David and David's intentions. He was 5-years old when he was dropped. For the next sixteen years he feared every time there was a knock on the door. Finally, when he was 21-years old, David came looking for him.

> David asked, "Is there anyone still left of the house of Saul... Ziba answered the king, "There is still a son of Jonathan; he is lame in both feet." ⁴"Where is he?" the king asked. Ziba answered, "He is at the house of Makir son of Ammiel in Lo Debar."—2 Samuel 9

The dreaded knock on the door had finally come for Mephibosheth. Life had been bad. He was crippled, living in the house of Makir (which means "to be sold"). Makir was the son of Ammiel (which means "darkness"). The town they live in was called Lo-debar (which means "A place of no pasture, a place of no promise, a dry place, a place of no bread"). But at least he was alive. Now, it looked like the end had finally come.

> ⁶When Mephibosheth son of Jonathan, the son of Saul, came to David, he bowed down to pay him honor. David said, "Mephibosheth!" At your service," he replied. "Don't be afraid," David said to him, "for I will surely show you kindness for the sake of your father Jonathan. I will restore to you all the land that belonged to your grandfather Saul, and you will always eat at my table."—2 Samuel 9:6-7

What?! Mephibosheth must've been stunned. I bet he couldn't believe his ears. If you had been in his shoes, what would you have thought? (Actually, I'm sure he didn't even have any shoes, but still. Put yourself in his place.)

> Mephibosheth bowed down and said, "What is your servant, that you should notice a dead dog like me?"—2 Samuel 9:8

Before the King, Mephibosheth believed he was nothing but a dead dog. He had lived for 16 years in fear and hiding from the King. But he didn't know what was going on in King David's heart. When he was invited to eat at the King's table, and that invitation opened up the unthinkable:

> Then the king summoned Ziba, Saul's steward, and said to him, "I have given your master's grandson everything that belonged to Saul and his family. You and your sons and your servants are to farm the land for him and bring in the crops, so that your master's grandson may be provided for. And Mephibosheth, grandson of your master, will always eat at my table." … So Mephibosheth ate at David's table like one of the king's sons. And Mephibosheth lived in Jerusalem, because he always ate at the king's table; he was lame in both feet. —2 Samuel 9:9-13

Hopefully, you are picking up the parallels between Mephibosheth's story and yours. Listen, the King of Kings is knocking on your door. He's inviting you to his table. You would have every reason to be afraid if the Bible hadn't already told you what was in Jesus' heart. He loves you, he died for you, and he wants you to walk with him and live with him every moment of every day, including dining with him at the table.

Not only does Jesus want to be *with* you at the table, but he says that he himself *is* the nourishment and the life that is served at the table.

FOOD FOR LIFE

Let's take a look at a major "table moment" that Jesus had with his followers. When I say "major" I mean "major". It involved a lot of people and a lot of food and when it was all said and done, Jesus used it as a segue to tell this disciples about a major, major spiritual truth.

Some time after this, Jesus crossed to the far shore of the Sea of Galilee (that is, the Sea of Tiberias), and a great crowd of people followed him because they saw the signs he had performed by healing the sick...When Jesus looked up and saw a great crowd coming toward him, he said to Philip, "Where shall we buy bread for these people to eat?"... Philip answered him, "It would take more than half a year's wages to buy enough bread for each one to have a bite!"

What happened next has become legendary. With five loaves of bread and two small fish borrowed from a young boy, Jesus fed the whole crew. Everybody full, happy and very impressed. They even wanted to make him their king. Jesus dodged that, then took a walk that on the water that evening, blowing his disciples' minds one more time.

[25] When they found him on the other side of the lake, they asked him, "Rabbi, when did you get here?"

Sure, these guys were stunned that Jesus power over the laws of the universe. But that's not what Jesus wanted to talk about. He had answers to questions that they weren't even asking yet. Jesus cut through their amazement and exposed the selfish motives that were lurking in their hearts.

[26] Jesus answered, "Very truly I tell you, you are looking for me, not because you saw the signs I performed but because you ate the loaves and had your fill. [27] Do not work for food that spoils, but for food that endures to eternal life, which the Son of Man will give you. For on him God the Father has placed his seal of approval." [28] Then they asked him, "What must we do to do the works God requires?" [29] Jesus answered, "The work of God is this: to believe in the one he has sent." [30] So they asked him, "What sign then will you give that we may see it and believe you? What will you do? [31] Our ancestors ate the manna in the wilderness; as it is written: 'He gave them bread from heaven to eat.'" [32] Jesus said to them, "Very truly I tell you, it is not Moses who has given you the bread from heaven, but it is my Father who gives you the true bread from heaven. [33] For the bread of

God is the bread that comes down from heaven and gives life to the world."[34] "Sir," they said, "always give us this bread." [35] Then Jesus declared, "I am the bread of life. Whoever comes to me will never go hungry, and whoever believes in me will never be thirsty. [40] For my Father's will is that everyone who looks to the Son and believes in him shall have eternal life, and I will raise them up at the last day." — John 6:25-40

There is some pretty heavy stuff in that passage. The most intense lesson (at least in my opinion) starts back when Jesus was feeding all of those people. They liked him for what he had done and what they hoped he would continue to do for them in the future. (Sound familiar?) They like him because he gave them bread, but then he said he *was* the bread-- but not the kind that spoils and leaves you hungry again, but an eternal type of bread that gave true spiritual life forever.

This is a major shift that takes us deeper still into the mysteries of the power of the table. Yes, physical tables are great places to feed our physical bodies and to engage in meaningful earthly relationships. That might be your motive for picking up this book: to have more and better earthly relationships with those who are important to you. Nothing wrong in that. In fact, I think that is awesome and I pray that the next 12 chapters will lead you to that. But in all honesty, that's not the end game. That's not even the real game plan. Jesus takes this whole "at the table" thing to an even deeper level with a deeper goal. He says, "Listen, you can want earthy stuff, but what I'm offering you is something more important, something that will never run out: *Me*. The bread of life. Eternal life. Right now."

AT THE TABLE WITH JESUS

It's really that simple. And I challenge you to not move ahead in this book until you've invited him in and dined with him at the table. So find a table somewhere where the two of you can be alone and then:

Ponder his words.

I'd suggest starting with his invitation in the letter to Laodicea in Revelation 3:14-20. Then, spent some time pondering his words in John 6:1-40. Really think about what he was saying to those people around him.

- In your opinion, what were the most important things that he was saying to the people who were with him or were receiving his message?
- If he communicated those same messages to you today, how would they impact you?

Share your heart.

Imagine that Christ is with you, sitting across the table. Because in a very real way, he really is. If you're alone where people can't hear you and think that you're psycho, talk out loud and share with him what's really going on in your heart.

- What are you thankful for?
- What are you fearful of?
- What are your dreams?

Then, listen for him to share his heart.

Jesus can speak directly to each and every one of us through the Bible, his written Word. Also, if you have opened the door of your life to him and accepted his invitation to come in to your heart, his Spirit can speak directly to your spirit (if he chooses to do so).

- What do you think he is telling you through his written words?
- Is he speaking anything to you in your spirit that goes along with his written words?
- Is there anything specific that you feel he is telling you to do or not do?

SETTING THE TABLE WITH OTHERS

Your time together will get deep soon enough. For starters, I'd keep it not only simple, but keep it safe too.

- First, get everyone together at a table somewhere.
- If they don't already know, tell them about *INEVITABLE*.
- Share a significant "table moment" from your own life.
- Ask everyone to share a couple of life-changing moments that have happened to them at different kinds of tables.
- Read a couple portions from this introduction about the importance of physical tables and relationships, and how Jesus calls us to his table where we experience him as the bread of life.
- Maybe finish with a quick prayer, asking God to help everyone see tables as a place where marriage, family and ministry can thrive in new ways.

TABLE 1: MARRIAGE

Leg #1: Love

"As the Father has loved me, so have I loved you. Now remain in my love... I have told you this so that my joy may be in you and that your joy may be complete. My command is this: Love each other as I have loved you. Greater love has no one than this: to lay down one's life for one's friend.

—John 15:9, 11-13

ineviTABLE [in-ev-i-t*uh*-b*uh*l] *adjective*
1. Sure to occur, happen, or come; unalterable.
2. Guaranteed success for every relationship when we pursue God at the table.

TO THE UNINFORMED people sitting in the booths around us, I must have looked like a giddy, babbling, twenty-year-old punk kid because, well, I guess I was a giddy, babbling, twenty-year-old punk kid. I was in an Olive Garden in South Bend, Indiana, and I had waited a short eternity for those moments at the table. She was sitting across from me—finally! I felt suspended in bliss as the earth temporarily stopped rotating and as every star in the universe twinkled in approval. Yeah, this was the end of a long road, but in my heart—which was overflowing with optimism, passion, and certainty—I knew that this was just the beginning. Man, I was in *love*.

1

We ordered the "Tour of Italy," a mixed assortment of food that matched the smorgasbord of words that spewed out of my face. We laughed a lot. We talked a lot. But, most importantly, I made a commitment to her right there. "I'm not going to pursue you physically or kiss you until we know we're supposed to be married, if that's the case," I said through the candlelight. "Cindy, I want to have the best marriage ever."

Unquestionably, this was one of the most powerful table moments in my life—and I didn't even know what a "table moment" was yet. All I knew was that the two of us were alone at last and we were at the table--and that I wanted the time together there to matter. In every major area of our lives (marriage, parenting and ministry) the health of our relationships can be measured by the manner in which we address the table. The more important the relationship, the more important the table. Through the high points, and in the low points, every relationship in our lives can be measured at the table (or by the fact that they are not at the table). When we come to the table as God intended, success is unavoidable—it's *inevitable*.

The most important leg under any relationship is love. Without it, a marriage, family and ministry always teeters on the edge of collapse. With love, the table stands firm, ready to fulfill its purpose to serve Christ, the bread of life, to those around us.

What is love? Just ask the apostle Paul. The Holy Spirit moved through Paul to write the Bible passage that is probably more quoted in more weddings than any other!

Love never gives up.
Love cares more for others than for self.
Love doesn't want what it doesn't have.
Love doesn't strut,
Doesn't have a swelled head,
Doesn't force itself on others,
Isn't always "me first,"
Doesn't fly off the handle,
Doesn't keep score of the sins of others,

Doesn't revel when others grovel,
Takes pleasure in the flowering of truth,
Puts up with anything,
Trusts God always,
Always looks for the best,
Never looks back,
But keeps going to the end.

—1 Corinthians 13:4-7 MSG

Words like that sound like music in the ears of all giddy punks sitting in Olive Gardens everywhere. But fast forward a couple years when you are sitting together at the dining room table. Forget the candles and the music. Food on the table of marriage seems bland—and then mix in some credit card debt, season it with some dirty diapers, and let it sit for a while in the middle of a lukewarm sexual relationship. Worse yet, the table of marriage exposes our bitter side like nothing else. Impatience, envy, pride, anger—marriage boils that to the surface. Pretty soon Paul's definition of love seems not only impractical, but maybe even impossible. Sound familiar? It does to me.

[12]My command is this: Love each other as I have loved you.[13]Greater love has no one than this: to lay down one's life for one's friends…[16]You did not choose me, but I chose you and appointed you so that you might go and bear fruit—fruit that will last—and so that whatever you ask in my name the Father will give you. [17]This is my command: Love each other. —John 15:12,13;16,17

Be honest with me now. You might read a passage like that and think *Yeah, right! I'm supposed to love like Jesus? Impossible.* And you know what? You are right.

This kind of love *is* impossible if (like most people) you are trying to love out of your own strength and your own emotions.

Please, I ask you to hit the brakes right now and stop and think for a moment. If you get this next passage of scripture, you'll get the key to love, the most important leg in any relationship. But if you miss it, you're likely to just roll your eyes and walk away from the table of marriage all together. Seriously, you might as well throw in the napkin and call it quits. If you want to experience the kind of love Jesus talked about in John 15, you have got to go back and ponder what he said in John 14.

> [15] "If you love me, keep my commands. [16] And I will ask the Father, and he will give you another advocate to help you and be with you forever— [17] the Spirit of truth… for he lives with you and will be in you. [18] I will not leave you as orphans; I will come to you…[21] Whoever has my commands and keeps them is the one who loves me. The one who loves me will be loved by my Father, and I too will love them and show myself to them."

> [22] Then Judas (not Judas Iscariot) said, "But, Lord, why do you intend to show yourself to us and not to the world?"[23] Jesus replied, "Anyone who loves me will obey my teaching. My Father will love them, and we will come to them and make our home with them…

> "I am the true vine, and my Father is the gardener. [4] Remain in me, as I also remain in you. No branch can bear fruit by itself; it must remain in the vine. Neither can you bear fruit unless you remain in me. [5] "I am the vine; you are the branches. If you remain in me and I in you, you will bear much fruit; apart from me you can do nothing. [8] This is to my Father's glory, that you bear much fruit, showing yourselves to be my disciples. [9] "As the Father has loved me, so have I loved you. Now remain in my love. [10] If you keep my commands, you will remain in my love, just as I have kept my Father's commands and remain in his love. [11] I have told you this so that my joy may be in you and that your joy may be complete. —John 14:15-17, 21-23 ; 15:1, 4-5, 8-11

There's a tremendous amount of meat in this passage, and you have a chance to chew on it at the end of this chapter. But for now, let me cut it up in the most important bite-sized chunks:

- Love is more important than anything else. It is the all-encompassing, universal command of God
- We are commanded to love like Jesus loved us (sacrificing our lives for others).
- Without Christ, you can't do *anything* of real value (particularly something as difficult as loving others like Christ loves you).
- The Holy Spirit is with you and lives in you to help you (if you have opened the door of your life to Christ).
- By "remaining" in Christ's love you will "bear much fruit."

Are you starting to see the word picture here? Marriage is like a table where you can serve the love of God to your spouse like a big bowl of fruit. That fruit only grows through a dependent, intimate relationship with Jesus Christ. If you feel like it's impossible to love your spouse right now, I get that. But that's because you're trying to love in your own strength rather than letting Christ love through you with his love.

> [14] For Christ's love compels us, because we are convinced that one died for all, and therefore all died. [15] And he died for all, that those who live should no longer live for themselves but for him who died for them and was raised again...[17] Therefore, if anyone is in Christ, the new creation has come: The old has gone, the new is here! [18] All this is from God, who reconciled us to himself through Christ and gave us the ministry of reconciliation.
> —2 Corinthians 5

> [13] I can do all this through him who gives me strength.
> —Philippians 4:13

Let me share with you what I want for my life: When people come to me for help, I want to be so full of God's love that they can dip into my life and drink deeply from the Spirit, and walk away changed in every way. I must stay full of God at all times; without him, I have nothing to offer. And without him, you have nothing to offer your spouse. He's the source of it all! You gotta tap into that source—or you have nothing to offer at the table.

> [7] Dear friends, let us love one another, for love comes from God. Everyone who loves has been born of God and knows God. [8] Whoever does not love does not know God, because God is love. [9] This is how God showed his love among us: He sent his one and only Son into the world that we might live through him.—1 John 4:7-9

It is *God's* love that flows through me, that's what makes me the best husband to Cindy that I can be. I'm telling you, it's the coolest thing possible: Cindy and I are one in Christ and together with God, we are strong. It *started* when we committed to morning Bible reading, prayer together every night, and an open line of transparent communication. These three things have made all the difference.

TABLES ON THEIR SIDES MAKE WALLS

Sometimes, marriage hits a wall. *We stayed married because we love God, not because we feel in love.* You want to be moving toward the table, you want to be growing, and deep inside you don't want to bail out, but then all of a sudden, "Blam!" Remember this truth: You smack into a concrete barrier and it seems like parts are flying everywhere and the whole mess explodes in a ball of flame. Listen, God wants you the table. But guess what? There is evil in this world, spiritual and physical forces that want to keep you away from dying with Christ and serving his love to your spouse. Satan is a liar. And he comes to steal kill and destroy the table. Here are some of the walls he builds in our world and in our minds:

Wall Number 1. "If this thing doesn't work for me, I'm out of here." Satan would like us to think that we can back away from the table of marriage and escape out the back door. But marriage is not a contract that can be broken anytime you feel like things are not going your way. Marriage is a covenant with God, and he wants you to stay at the table so you can experience true joy. You stay married not because you feel in love, but because you love God.

Remember: When you smash into the wall of hopelessness, the love of Christ in you can bust through!

Wall Number 2. "Women are from Venus and men are from Mars." Hello!? Of course men and women are different! Sheesh, just look at the different way our bodies are designed and then go from there. God *made* men and women different. But that's not an excuse to drift away and live at your own corners of the universe. God designed you to live together, with all your differences, right here on the same planet. If you are willing, you can discover this unity at the table.

Remember: When you impact the wall of differences, the love of Christ in you can bust through!

Wall number 3. The Headache. You've heard the line, "Not tonight honey, I have a headache." Well here's the plan guys: Bring two aspirins and a glass of water into the bedroom, hand them to her. She will say, "What are these for? I don't have a headache." Then you say, "Sweet! Then let's get some candles and light it up!"

If you're cutting your spouse off from sex on a regular basis, you're cutting away little pieces of their heart every time. But it's not just about sex. We say "Not now honey" in lots of different ways, and each time it communicates rejection. "Not now honey, I am busy coaching… I have to work late… I have a church meeting… I have to fold the laundry… I'm watching TV." Seriously guys, how many hours do we waste zoning out in front of worthless junk on the tube with the remote, *click… click… click…* Maybe it's time to shut the stupid thing off and figure out what makes our wives "click?"

The two of you were created to be intimate together emotionally, spiritually, and physically. Are you shaming your spouse by saying "no"?

When you continually say "no" to intimacy, you are refusing fellowship with God, because intimacy with your spouse is worship to God and it can happen at the table.

Remember: When your marriage is constantly running into "headaches", the love of Christ in you can break through.

Wall Number 4. K.I.D.S. (Keeping Intimacy Distanced Successfully) I'm all for awesome parenting. Kids are near the top God's priority list, but your spouse comes above them. If you let your kids dominate your marriage, everyone is likely to crash and burn. And it's not just kids. Your work, hobbies and church life must come after your commitment to spending quality time with each other. You need time and space for the two of you, and you can find that at the table.

Remember: When you hit the wall of kids, all you *really* need is a half-decent babysitter.

What I'm saying is that if you want to try to get to the table with your spouse, you better get used to busting through some walls. Satan, society, and even your own fears are going to build barriers to try to keep you away. Don't back off. Trust in Christ in you. He can bust through.

THE PROPOSAL AT THE TABLE

24 months after Olive Garden, I was on a ministry team in Mississippi. They were good months. When I knew it was time.

I spent at least $49.00 on that ring. I could easily see the rock on it from two feet away or less.

Cindy was 8 1/2 hours away on a ministry project in Little Rock, Arkansas. It was time to ask the most important question of my life. And it was going to happen at the table.

The couple phone calls, I got everything scripted with the host family at the home she and her team were staying with. When she came in that night, they said, "Hey, we're going to go ahead and go to bed. Do you mind shutting off the light in the kitchen for us?" But when she walked in, she saw Bible next to a candle on a small table in the center of the room—a Bible with my name on it. I heard her take a breath and she started looking around. I came out of a back room where I had been hiding, and—let me tell you— I can still remember the way she felt when I held her in my arms. The way her hair laid on her shoulders, the smell of her perfume; I remember everything.

Then I knelt down by the table in front of her, and looked into her eyes and asked, "Would you spend the rest of your life with me?" We started bawling, as I tried to get the ring box out of my pocket. "Okay, so I had gained a couple extra pounds in the months we've been apart, and didn't have the change to buy a bigger pair pants.) I put that ring on her finger and kissed her for the very first time. I made a vow to her that we would not kiss her until I asked her to marry me, but after I got that done we majorly made up for some lost time. As a matter of a fact, a little bit of razor stubble on my chin rubbed her chin till she had a little raw red strawberry. As our tears mixed with the warmth of that kiss.

I read to her a passage of Scripture that God had given me:

> [7] You husbands in the same way, live with your wives in an understanding way, as with someone weaker, since she is a woman; and show her honor as a fellow heir of the grace of life, so that your prayers will not be hindered.
>
> [8] To sum up, all of you be harmonious, sympathetic, brotherly, kindhearted, and humble in spirit; [9] not returning evil for evil or insult for insult, but giving a blessing instead; for you were called for the very purpose that you might inherit a blessing.
> —1 Peter 3:7-9 (NASB)

I wish I could say I've always obeyed it. But I haven't. There's been evil and insults and there have been times that I have deeply wounded Cindy rather than showing her honor. If not for forgiveness, I don't know where we would be. But I've never forgotten that passage or the night I proposed to Cindy at the table. That was a major step. So I'm going to propose something to you right now. I'm going to propose that you step up to the table and make a decision to serve up some love and honor to your spouse.

SERVING THE LOVE OF CHRIST TO YOUR SPOUSE

Men, let me start with you. We're called to honor our wives and treat them with understanding "as with someone weaker." But get this right: Weaker doesn't mean less significant. We're talking about the difference between is the difference between steel and gold, clay and porcelain and clay, denim and silk. Most importantly, she is a "fellow heir of the grace of life." Gentlemen, that means that she is a daughter of the King of kings and the Lord of Lords and she should be treated that way.

Ten Ways a Man can Honor a Woman

1) **Prioritize Christ.** How does that happen? Through prayer, pondering the Bible and listening to what Christ is telling you to do. Your relationship with Christ as the source and the foundation of all your other relationships. Make him number one.
2) **Lead in Shaping our Kids.** Have a unified vision in discipline, direction, and devotion to Jesus Christ.
3) **Lead spiritually.** I know that is scary, and I know you might feel in adequate. But it's worth it in Christ in you can do it. We'll show you how the rest of the book.
4) **Defend her.** Defend her physically, emotionally, socially, and spiritually. You are the man. Protect and defend her, particularly where she is weaker.
5) **Give her the passwords.** Separate accounts breed separate lives. Give her access. Let her in. That's bank accounts, social media, mobile devices, and e-mail. I know there might be some damaging stuff in there but it's time to be honest and transparent.

6) **Serve her.** Think about where you can make her feel special and pampered and do it. Maybe pick the thing that she hates, man up, and do it yourself.

7) **Tell her.** You'll get more about this in the communication chapter, but for now find a unique way to tell heard about just one thing that you like and love about her.

8) **Say "yes" and mean it.** You said yes at the altar. Slide up to the table and turn your back on the door. Burn your bridges and remove the girl at work from your Facebook friend list.

9) **Touch her.** Do it in front of your kids. Kiss her on the mouth and hug her when you head out the door in the morning, not just when you hope to get lucky at night.

10) **Date her.** She is still your girlfriend so plan a great table date and make it a weekly habit.

Okay, women, your turn. If you want to know how to honor a man, be feminine strong. Proverbs 14:1 says "The wise woman builds her house, but with her own hands the foolish one tears hers down." That's strong stuff, and the Scriptures are full of examples of women who show this kind of strength. Study women like Deborah. She was God-fearing, she recognized the leadership in her home. She lead and was unbelievable. Jael worked with Deborah—she is the one that went into the tent, drove the tent peg in an enemy guy's head. And Esther, she saved a whole nation because she was willing to face death for what was right. If you want some bullet points about how to honor a man through feminine strength, look at Proverbs 31.

Ten ways a woman can honor a man:

1) **Be full of faith.** It's your relationship with God that will be your strength. Keep God number one in your life so that he can live through you to love others as he love

2) **Be trustworthy.** Say it and do it. It's that simple.

3) **Make marriage a priority.** Put your man on your to do list. Commit to making your relationship better. Be willing to let

Christ love your husband through you. You may have to take the first move on this if your husband isn't ready to come to the table yet.

4) **Be serious about your time.** Manage your time well so that your highest priorities are at the top of the endless list of things that you need to get done and the insignificant stuff that saps your energy and time don't.

5) **Be aware of your finances**. Don't go into neutral. Yes, there could be a situation where your husband is in charge ultimately of the overall financial situation of the home, but do you can to assist him and know what's going on-- and encouraged him and affirm him when money is tight. It's hard on a guy and he could really use your support.

6) **Be serious about mothering**. Those kids will be your family's legacy, and your family's legacy will honor your husband.

7) **Serve big-time.** I love going into a home where the wife is serious about serving the husband. Do you want to see a picture of God's church illuminated like never before? Be that wife. It's a beautiful, beautiful picture.

8) **Have an entrepreneurial spirit.** You can initiate things and create things that wouldn't exist without you. Never hesitate to step out in new ways in your marriage.

9) **Be a giver.** Nothing will crush your marriage faster than greed. The Lord will supply all your needs. You can give the best of what you have, what you can do, and who you are to your husband.

10) **Burn the Honey-not-tonight gown.** Yeah! And while you're at it, torch the "granny panties." When you dress down for the night, dress it up for him. That will honor him in ways you probably can't even imagine.

Cindy and I have learned a lot about honoring each other in the last 20 years. Most of it didn't come naturally, and a lot of that we never even would've thought about on our own. Listen, I still cherish that table moment in Olive Garden. For our 18th anniversary I took her back to that restaurant, but it's different now. Sure, we have made it a top priority to make romantic evenings are regular item on our marriage menu, but our love is *deeper*. The flame still burns bright for us and candles still flicker all the time but it comes from a deep bed of coals of glowing love; it's the love of God heating it all up.

Marriage is not a moment of passion. It's a momentous covenant call of God. You have to be reminded of that calling, because just like your walk with Christ, it's going to be eb and flow, up and down, heaven and hell, drought and downpour. If it's rough and you are ready to bail, I get that. If it's just tough, and you're feeling really drained at the marriage table, I get that too. Maybe your marriage is doing okay, but you're ready to make the move from "good to great", or "great to awesome."

No matter where you are in your marriage, remember what Jesus did at the very beginning of his ministry at a wedding. When they ran out of supplies, naturally it looked like the party was over. But Jesus did something supernatural: he went to the table, took ordinary bland water and turned it into wine—but not just *any* wine, it was *fine* wine, the *best* wine that they had been served that night.

Maybe you are in need of a miracle too. Believe it or not, Jesus in you can do the impossible. Just remember, the first miracle of Jesus happened at a wedding, and it happened at the table.

Lord Jesus,

Thank you for coming into my life and dining with me. Thank you for putting your Holy Spirit in me so I can know your love and so you can love others through me. I agree with your scriptures that say I can do nothing apart from you. So I ask you to show me how you want to honor and bless my spouse and all people around me. Fill me with hope, give me the willingness to obey, for I believe that you are the God of love and miracles.

Amen

AT THE TABLE

Find a table where you can experience the presence of Christ and his Holy Spirit without distraction or interruption. I believe he has a lot to tell you through his Word and through his Spirit.

Ponder John 14-15. Really think about God's love for you. John wrote that "we love because he first loved us." Ask God to make these passages come alive to you so that God's love for you is etched firmly in your heart.

Pray with honesty. I mean, really pour your heart out about where you are in your marriage.

Ponder 1 Peter 3. A lot of deep stuff here. Let it soak in.

Listen to his lead. Through the Bible and through his spirit, I believe he will give you direction, hope, and even show you the specific ways that he wants you to honor and bless your spouse.

AT THE TABLE WITH YOUR SPOUSE

Carve out a special time at the table with your mate. Why don't you pick one of their favorite places to go? But give it some thought ahead of time. Pray through the list of "10 ways you can honor your spouse." Seriously consider the different ways that you bless your spouse at the table at that time. Be willing to follow Christ's lead no matter how crazy or uncomfortable it might seem. You're charting new ground here. You may not do it perfectly, and it might be awkward. Your spouse might not even receive it, but go for it! You're serving the love of Christ to your spouse at the table of marriage.

Table 1: Marriage

Leg #2: Forgiveness

> God made you alive with Christ. He forgave us all our sins, having canceled the charge of our legal indebtedness, which stood against us and condemned us; he has taken it away, nailing it to the cross.
>
> —Colossians 2:13-14

turnTABLE [turn-tey-b*uh*l] *noun*
1. The rotating disk that spins the record on a phonograph.
2. The 180-degree shift a relationship can make when forgiveness frees people to be who they are in Christ.

I am not Jesus. (Now there's a revelation! Aren't you glad you bought this book?) But sometimes, people think a pastor should be more like Jesus than other mere mortals. The fact is, we are just dudes with all the doubts and struggles and temptations as a normal Joe. One night early in our marriage, that was graphically obvious. I was still doing the youth pastor gig. Great job. I loved it. But one of the young women in our group was shopping for love in all the wrong places and she was selling everything that she had to get it. I wish I could be more spiritual about it, but I'm just telling it like it was.

We had the no PDA (public display of affection) rule in our group, but we did allow the "side-hug." That night she gave me the side-hug and I side-hugged her back—ministry stuff, right? I'm affirming this gal, just letting her know her value before God, encouraging her in her walk with Christ... and then, the twist. We pivoted in a way that pressed her chest to mine. It only lasted a second or two, but it felt like minutes—and in all honesty, at that moment, every molecule of my flesh wished it could last for hours. I allowed myself to be carried away by lust, and the lust gave birth to full-blown sin in my mind.

It took a little while to shake it off. Later that night I confessed it to God, vowed to keep my distance from her and move on. *Praise the Lord. No harm done. Nobody knows. Nobody needs to know. Just forget it.*

Fast forward 3 1/2 months. I was officiating a revival meeting of all things. A lot of people were there, it was a big spiritual mountaintop type of deal. I was sitting next to Cindy thinking about how I was going to close the meeting. *"Thanks for being here! Wow didn't God speak to us tonight, Hallelujah, Glory to God. Amen brother! Halleluiah! Somebody say amen!"* Yeah, that would wrap it up, we would take an offering, and everybody would think I was awesome.

But then I heard it, that quiet voice that sometimes shouts in our souls. "Shannon, remember that girl? You have to tell Cindy right now that you lusted."

"Thanks God, but I need to close this service. I will get on that later, okay?" I prayed.

I tried to refocus on what was happening around me and prepare for what I was going to do, but the dodge didn't work. It's a little hard to fake God out. The voice of the Spirit wouldn't shut up and this time God's conviction hit full force. Feelings of guilt rushed through my veins. I didn't want to tell her at all, of course, but now? When I'm leading a revival? That was out of the question.

"Lord, you want me to tell my wife that I had sex in my mind with a teenage girl?! Now!?"

"Shannon you need to clear your conscience. If you can't share and clear your conscience here with your earthly bride, then how are you going to be able to walk with your groom Jesus?"

Seriously, it felt like everything in the room froze. The speaker was still speaking but I couldn't hear it. People were all around but it was like I couldn't see them. Everything inside of me wanted to deny and ignore it. There was just too much at stake. We had only been married three years. This could crush her. I could see her running from the room. I could see myself hitchhiking home and finding my stuff scattered all over the front lawn.

Nothing would be the same after this. For better or for worse, what God was asking would turn the table of our relationship.

Cindy taught me that day that we do not stay married because we feel in love, but because we love God.

A LONG TIME AGO, IN A GARDEN FAR, FAR AWAY

After God finished creating the heavens and the earth and filling it with plants and animals and the first man, God said it was "good". After he created Eve, however, and put her together with Adam he called it "very good". The scripture says that the man and the woman were naked and they were not ashamed. (I say "Amen! Praise God for that.")

But just a few verses ahead, Adam and Eve rejected God's perfectly created order and disobeyed the boundaries that he had created for their protection. BLAM! Just like that everything changed. Innocence was lost. Purity was defiled, and "they were ashamed because they were naked." (Genesis 2) They suddenly realized that they were naked and they were ashamed. The implications of this one act were cataclysmic. It was a 10.0 earthquake on the relationship scale. Unity with God was broken and their relationship with each other quickly dissolved into a fearful game of blame. It was a natural consequence:

Whenever sin lives, intimacy dies.

We all struggle with intimacy issues with God and others. But you may be thinking, "Shannon, I don't have any big sins." Really? You must realize that any sin is sin. Take pride for instance, when you become prideful, intimacy dies. I know that many of you are asking, "Why is there no intimacy in our marriage? Where did it go? Why is he no longer pursuing me?" If sin is allowed to live, it will kill your relationship. Even secret sins that only live in your head will destroy intimacy with your spouse. When sin lives, intimacy dies not only with your spouse, but also with God, your kids, your friends, your parents... everyone.

With so much sin living around us, in us, and between us, is it ever possible that we could be naked and unashamed again? The answer can be found "at the table."

[36] When one of the Pharisees invited Jesus to have dinner with him, he went to the Pharisee's house and reclined at the table. [37] A woman in that town who lived a sinful life learned that Jesus was eating at the Pharisee's house, so she came there with an alabaster jar of perfume. [38] As she stood behind him at his feet weeping, she began to wet his feet with her tears. Then she wiped them with her hair, kissed them and poured perfume on them.

Okay, if you're looking for a really intense "Jesus at the table moment" this is it! He's hanging out with the bigwigs' religious guys. These guys kept every rule possible to avoiding sin, and they had this elaborate system of sacrifices to cleanse themselves when they did sin. And now a prostitute was throwing herself at Jesus, kissing his feet?!

[39] When the Pharisee who had invited him saw this, he said to himself, "If this man were a prophet, he would know who is touching him and what kind of woman she is—that she is a sinner."

Check this out: the Pharisee was saying this "to himself," but Jesus heard it loud and clear. And he answered with a story... a story that should give hope to all of us who experience the broken intimacy caused by sin.

[40] Jesus answered him, "Simon, I have something to tell you." "Tell me, teacher," he said. [41] "Two people owed money to a certain moneylender. One owed him five hundred denarii, and the other fifty. [42] Neither of them had the money to pay him back, so he forgave the debts of both. Now which of them will love him more?" [43] Simon replied, "I suppose the one who had the bigger debt forgiven." "You have judged correctly," Jesus said. [44] Then he turned toward the woman and said to Simon, "Do you see this woman? I came into your house. You did not give me any water for my feet, but she wet my feet with her tears

and wiped them with her hair. [45] You did not give me a kiss, but this woman, from the time I entered, has not stopped kissing my feet. [46] You did not put oil on my head, but she has poured perfume on my feet. [47] Therefore, I tell you, her many sins have been forgiven—as her great love has shown. But whoever has been forgiven little loves little." [48] Then Jesus said to her, "Your sins are forgiven."[49] The other guests began to say among themselves, "Who is this who even forgives sins?" [50] Jesus said to the woman, "Your faith has saved you; go in peace."

—Luke 7:36-50

I, for one, think that rocks. What happened at the table that night set the stage for what was to play out on a cross outside Jerusalem shortly after this dinner. Jesus not only received a notorious sinner, but he knew what to do with her sin… and my sin, and yours.

[13] When you were dead in your sins and in the uncircumcision of your flesh, God made you alive with Christ. He forgave us all our sins,[14] having canceled the charge of our legal indebtedness, which stood against us and condemned us; he has taken it away, nailing it to the cross.—Colossians 2:13-14

This is one powerful word picture, and it's based on what really happened. God took your sins and he killed them. He nailed them to the cross with Jesus. Can you see it? Can you imagine your sins being pounded onto the rough wood beams where Jesus hung and died? Forgiveness is the divine transaction, paid in full by the blood of Jesus, which frees both the offender and the offended from the bondage of sin:

Whenever sin dies, intimacy lives!

But let me back up for a moment, because many of us have lived in denial and repression of our sin. Why? My guess is that most of us don't know how to handle our sin. And without forgiveness, it's just too much to handle, so we stuff it away somewhere in our soul. The first step in healing broken intimacy is sincerely recognizing what you have done. And it's is not just what you have done, it's also what you have thought and said.

> [8] If we claim to be without sin, we deceive ourselves and the truth is not in us. [9] If we confess our sins, he is faithful and just and will forgive us our sins and purify us from all unrighteousness. [10] If we claim we have not sinned, we make him out to be a liar and his word is not in us. —1 John 1:8-9

When forgiveness flows, sin dies and intimacy flourishes. Forgiveness unleashes a freedom that sets the captives free.

FEEDING ON GOD'S FORGIVENESS

The restoration of intimacy starts when you get real with God, and let his forgiveness flow into your life first. Then that forgiveness can flow to others and start healing your relationships. The Bible shows the steps to get you there:

1. **Get transparent**. God knows everything. We might as well be honest. His Word and his Spirit in you will reveal specific sins that he wants to deal with.
   Search me, God, and know my heart; test me and know my anxious thoughts. See if there is any offensive way in me, and lead me in the way everlasting. —Psalm 139:23-24

2. **Agree.** When you accept as true what the Holy Spirit reveals about your sin, the Father forgives you and the blood of Jesus has cleanses you from guilt and shame.
   If we confess our sins, he is faithful and just and will forgive us our sins and purify us from all unrighteousness.—1 John 1:9

3. **Imagine.** Close your eyes and see God taking that list of your sins and nailing it to the cross where Jesus is hanging.

...having canceled the charge of our legal indebtedness, which stood against us and condemned us; he has taken it away, nailing it to the cross. —Colossians 2:14

4. **Praise God**! Worship God for what he has done and soak in the intimacy of your relationship with him again.
Blessed is the one whose transgressions are forgiven, whose sins are covered.—Psalm 32:1

FORGIVING OTHERS

Several years ago, Cindy, my wife, had an affair. She didn't *do* anything inappropriate—no sexual contact, and she never even met with the guy in private. It was an affair of the heart—an emotional connection with another man where she began to feed off his affection and attention. When the Sprit convicted her, she knew that she had crossed the line: this was emotional adultery. She came to me with that, and I'm telling you, it hit me hard and it hurt me deep.

I had a choice now. I could either wallow in that pain letting it fester into bitterness, resentment and anger, or I could release it to God, be free, and begin healing. It seems like an obvious choice. In all honesty, it's not an easy an easy one to make. Pride is such a powerful thing, but thankfully the truth of God and the power of his Spirit in us is stronger.

Get rid of all bitterness, rage and anger, brawling and slander, along with every form of malice. Be kind and compassionate to one another, **forgiving each other, just as in Christ God forgave you.**—Ephesians 4:31-32

Let me make something clear, though. Forgiveness does not mean forgetting. And it doesn't mean that you return to an abusive situation. And it doesn't mean that there won't be natural consequences for the other person. Forgiveness frees *you* from the anger and bitterness caused by *their* actions. When you've been wounded, forgiveness is the only way to healing. But how can you forgive others like Christ forgave us? You can't (just like you can't love like God loves) but Christ in you can. Here's how:

1. **Remember.** Get real with God. You'll need to "embrace the wrong" that has happened to you. Don't deny it or suppress it or make excuses for the one who hurts you.
2. **Trust.** Recognize that true forgiveness only happens when you rely on Christ to forgive through you. You'll really need to activate your mind to do this. Forgiveness is a choice, not an emotion.

   I can do all this through him who gives me strength.—Philippians 4:13

3. **Release.** Pray, "Jesus, thank you for forgiving me. I let go of the pain that this has caused and will not hold it against them. You are just. I trust you to punish them if you say that is appropriate."

   Do not take revenge, my dear friends, but leave room for God's wrath, for it **is** written: "It **is mine** to avenge; I will repay," says the Lord.
   —Romans 12:19

4. **Bless.** Listen, I know this one sounds crazy at first, but the full healing power of forgiveness is unleashed when you turn around and do something that blesses the person who hurt you. When you do something right for someone who has wronged you, you shatter the division that Satan wants to see in relationships and you take a major step towards the intimacy and healing that God designed.

   Finally, all of you, be like-minded, be sympathetic, love one another, be compassionate and humble. ⁹ Do not repay evil with evil or insult with insult. On the contrary, repay evil with blessing, because to this you were called so that you may inherit a blessing. —1 Peter 3:8-9

REQUESTING FORGIVENESS FROM OTHERS

It's one thing to be wounded; it's another thing to be the one who has caused the wound. The way to be free from the mental and emotional weight of your sin against someone else is to seek their forgiveness. I'm not saying this is easy. I am saying it's required. It's so important that Jesus said this process should even interrupt your normal worship routine.

> "Therefore, if you are offering your gift at the altar and there remember that your brother or sister has something against you, ²⁴ leave your gift there in front of the altar. First go and be reconciled to them; then come and offer your gift."
>
> —Matthew 5:23-24

The process of asking for forgiveness is fairly simple, as you will see in a second. But let me advise you: If you need to ask for forgiveness for something seriously major that your spouse doesn't know about, I would recommend talking with a pastor or a professional counselor beforehand. They will pray with you and help you pull together a plan to bring what you have done to the table. Cindy and I *regularly* go to a professional counselor to mediate in our relationship. A lot of people have personal trainers and business consultants. Cindy I know that our relationship is far more important than our bodies or bucks, so we find the best help we can. A pro will help you walk through it.

How to request forgiveness

1. **Recognize.** Let God search your heart and show you your ways. And then see your sin for what it is. Own up to it. Be responsible for it.
2. **Thank.** Let God know that you deeply appreciate his forgiveness. Ultimately, all sin is against God, and his forgiveness cleanses you and frees you from the things you have done against others.

3. **Ask.** When the time comes, tell the person specifically what you know you did to wrong them. Tell them you are sorry that you did it. And then say the four hardest words to say: *Will you forgive me?*

4. **Be free.** Asking for forgiveness doesn't necessarily mean that you're going to get forgiveness. With God, forgiveness is guaranteed. With people, you never know. Sometimes it takes a while before people are willing to let Christ forgive though them. Sometimes it never happens. The person you hurt might even go to the grave holding on to the pain you caused. That's hard, but it's out of your hands. Either way you should willingly accept the natural consequences of your actions and then move on knowing that God nailed those sins to the cross.

Therefore, there is now no condemnation for those who are in Christ Jesus, [2] because through Christ Jesus the law of the Spirit who gives life has set you free from the law of sin and death.—Romans 8:1-2

HEALING *NOW*

I can still remember the emotions and feelings that were tearing through my soul and my body that day at the revival meeting, when God told me that I needed to tell Cindy and request her forgiveness for the lust I had embraced for that teenage girl. I could feel myself beginning to shake inside and sweat on the outside.

"God, I can't tell her that. She's gonna leave me. I, I just can't, not right now."

And I was partly right. *I* couldn't do it. But Christ in me could if I let him. And my stalling techniques weren't working anyway. I knew better than that. Delayed obedience is disobedience. So I took a deep breath and the words started to flow from my mouth.

"Babe, I need to talk to you about something."

"Sure. Okay," she said, waiting.

"No," I said. "We need to get on our knees and you need to put your hands behind your back." We knelt right there on the front row.

"Cindy, I lusted in my heart for another woman…" I told her the whole situation. She was quiet for a few seconds (which is rarely good) but I knew at that moment the timing was right. The Spirit of God told me to do exactly what I did. Now it was out of my control. Cindy looked over at me and put her arm around my shoulders and pulled me close, I can still almost even smell her sweet breath on my cheek.

She looked right at me and said, "Babe, I love you more right now than I have ever loved you."

I started to cry. When I looked at her, I *saw* Cindy, but then a powerful realization rushed over me. I was *looking* at Jesus. It was Jesus in her, forgiving me through her, because one day he was scourged, beaten until he was unrecognizable as a human. . It was Jesus saying "I love you more now than ever. I love you more now than ever." It was Jesus in her that willingly hung on the cross, bleeding there for me until he could barely breathe, finally gasping, "It is finished" *Tetelestai!* Paid in full. Cindy had taken my sin to the cross where God crucified it with Christ.

And then, Christ rose again… and so did Cindy and I. We slowly stood up together more powerful, more anointed, more ready to do ministry than we ever had before when I sat there and I lied to her in my silence. The transparency brought unbelievable relational beauty. Sin had died and intimacy lived.

Cindy's emotional affair and my lust for a teenaged girl could have been the end of our relationship—but forgiveness brought new life to us instead. Those two moments are some of the most powerful moments in our entire marriage. It was humbling, terrifying, and could have meant the death of our intimacy. But forgiveness flowed and it brought about some of the greatest beauty that our marriage has ever experienced.

When sin dies at the cross of forgiveness, get ready for the resurrection in your marriage.

Forgiveness is always the new beginning of a deep intimacy. God forgives us completely and entirely, he died for sins once and for all. The process of putting his forgiveness to use marriage never ends. This is a new way of life! Thank God for his forgiveness; forgive others, and seek forgiveness from others. Because when sin tries to kill your intimacy, you can put it to death on the cross time after time after time with forgiveness.

My God,

I believe that you are the God of forgiveness. By the power of your Holy Spirit in me, I ask that forgiveness would flow to me and through me. With all my heart, I am eternally thankful for your forgiveness. Empower me to forgive others. Give me the courage to seek forgiveness from those I have sinned against. Together, let's nail all that sin to the cross and let it die, so that intimacy will live in my relationship with you, my mate, and everyone you have placed in my life.

Amen.

AT THE TABLE WITH JESUS.

Before you sit down to have some focused time with Christ at the table, do a very simple arts and crafts project: Make a cross! Cardboard works fine but you'll need some extra staples or pins. Two pieces of wood would work too if you have a couple of extra nails. Seriously, do it! We are going to crucify some sin.

ALL relationships need regular forgiveness to free them for intimacy. You'll want to go through the following steps for each important person in your life. But since this is the marriage section, start with you mate.

Ponder
Spend some time soaking in Colossians 2. That chapter is filled with sin-slaughtering truth. Underline and circle the passages that the Holy Spirit emphasizes for you.

Pray
Read the words of Psalm 139, but make this prayer of David your prayer. Go through it thought by thought, sharing your thoughts with God. Ask him to show you how you have sinned against your spouse.

Listen

1. **Get transparent**. Be honest with yourself and God as his Word and his Spirit reveal specific sins that he wants to deal with.
2. **Agree.** Accept as true what the Holy Spirit reveals about your sin toward your spouse. WRITE THEM DOWN.
3. **Imagine**. Close your eyes and see God taking that list of your sins and nailing it to the cross where Jesus is hanging. THEN ACTUALLY DO IT. Nail you list of sins to the cross you made. Know that God really put those sins to death on the cross of Christ.
4. **Praise God**! Worship God for what he has done and soak in the intimacy of your relationship with him. Forgiveness awesome. Be free in what he has done for you!

Now, let's walk through it again, but this time you will release yourself from the sins your spouse has committed against you.

Ponder
Spend some time thinking about Ephesians 4. Skim the whole chapter, marking it up as you go along. Pay close attention to verses 28-32.

Pray
Ask the Holy Spirit to guide you and empower you to deal with the pain and hurt your mate has caused.

1. **Remember**. Embrace the wrong that your spouse has done to you. GO AHEAD AND MAKE A LIST.
2. **Trust.** You *can* forgive through Christ who gives you strength. Tell God you are depending on him to make you willing and able.
3. **Release**. Pray through each item. "Jesus, thank you for forgiving me. I let go of the pain that this has caused and will not hold it against them. You are just. I trust you to punish them if you think it is appropriate." When you are all done, DESROY THIS LIST. Unless your spouse specifically asks for your forgiveness for these things, you don't even need to tell them they are forgiven.

4. **Bless.** You know the things that mean the most to your spouse. Ask God to help you pick one special way to bless them, then do it ASAP.

AT THE TABLE WITH YOUR SPOUSE

Ideally, both you and your spouse are now going through this book together. If so, set a date at a table in a very private place. Be praying for your time together. You might want to fast for a period of time. Be sure you have your table time alone with Christ before you come together. This is holy ground, the real deal. I know it sounds awkward and strange, but if you want to see resurrection in your marriage, the death of sin through radical forgiveness is how you do it.

When you come together at the table, bring the cross as you made and the list of sins that you have committed against your spouse.

Ponder
Read Romans 8:1-12 together.

Pray
Ask God to put sin to death in your marriage.

1. **Recognize.** Take turns sharing your list of sins against each other. Make no excuses. Own up to it. Be responsible for it.
2. **Thank.** Let them know that you believe God has forgiven you for and that you have thanked him and praised him for it.
3. **Ask.** Tell them you are sorry that you did it. And then say the four hardest words to say: *Will you forgive me?*
4. **Be free.** Take the list of sins your spouse has confessed to you and nail them to your cross. Then, together, praise God for taking all the sins to the cross and crucifying them. DESTROY THE LISTS TOGETHER.

And one last thing. Back in the garden, before sin entered the equation, Adam and Eve were "naked and not ashamed." The blood of Jesus has wiped away our sin and shame. When the two of you embrace that forgiveness, sin dies, and intimacy is resurrected. Getting shamelessly naked together is a great way to celebrate. Just an idea…

AT THE TABLE WITH A DISCUSSION GROUP

1. Circle or underline the most important things you read in this chapter. Why did you pick these things?
2. Do you think it is possible for a person to be forgiven by God, but not feel it or believe it? Why or why not?
3. If you have sinned against someone, but it has caused them no pain and they aren't even aware, do you think you are required to confess it to that person if God doesn't specifically tell you do so? Explain why you feel this way.
4. Do you know of a situation where someone asked for forgiveness but it wasn't given? If so, what were the long term consequences of this choice?
5. Do you think it is possible to forgive a sin without "nailing it to the cross"?

What are you basing your answer on?

Table 1: Marriage

Leg #3: Communication

> And this is my prayer: that your love may abound more and more in knowledge and depth of insight, [1]so that you may be able to discern what is best and may be pure and blameless for the day of Christ, filled with the fruit of righteousness that comes through Jesus Christ—to the glory and praise of God.

> —Philippians 1:9-11

sTABLE [stey-bu*h*l] *adjective*
1. Not likely to fall or give way, as a structure, support or a foundation. Able to continue or last; enduring and permanent
2. Relationships that are built on awesome communication that takes place across a table.

Cindy was frustrated. She was trying to tell me I wasn't listening to her—at least I think that's what she said. I wasn't really paying attention. I saw her mouth moving and the sound of her voice was bouncing around somewhere in my head, but it just wasn't connecting with my brain (so it sure wasn't connecting with my heart either).

I'm a pastor, I get paid to talk, not listen. I'm a professional *speaker...* But that doesn't mean I'm a good *communicator.* Talking comes easy. But when it comes to communication, one of the four essential legs beneath a table of marriage, I'm a piece of work, and I need to work at it. And you know what? It's worth the work. Communication in marriage is not just a back-and-forth exchange of ideas. The *process* is an extension of the oneness that God created between a man and a woman way back in Eden.

> [2]Then the Lord God made a woman from the rib he had taken out of the man, and he brought her to the man. [23]The man said, "This is now bone of my bones and flesh of my flesh; she shall be called 'woman,' for she was taken out of man." [24]That is why

a man leaves his father and mother and is united to his wife, and they become one flesh.—Genesis 2:2, 23-24

How many times have you "won" an argument with your spouse only to realize the both of you have lost? Why is that? It's because you're arguing with yourself, because the two of you are one. When you stiff arm your spouse? You're stiff arming yourself, because the two of you are one. When you criticize your spouse? Yep, you just do it to yourself. That's why it feels so awful afterwards, even when you appear to have gotten the upper hand.

And some of the stuff we argue over? It's just crazy! "You took my keys." "No, I didn't." "Yes, you did. I guarantee you had them last." "No I didn't!!!" "Yes you did!!! And then next thing you know, it's like Mount St. Helens blows up in your living room—and then you do find the car keys in your own pocket. (I hate it when that happens!) Well, you might as well just drive on down to the attorney's office and get started on the divorce papers. Okay, maybe not exactly. You don't end up in divorce court over one incident like that. And you don't just decide one afternoon to jump in bed with the person working in the cubicle next to you that night. No, it's 10,000 itty-bitty steps that get you there. And every step of the way, there was a breakdown in the way God designed communication to work to unify your marriage.

We all started off better than that. I remember one time I bought Cindy a cheap sweater at Wal-Mart. Then I got some puffy paint and wrote her a letter on the front of the shirt. I misspelled two words (really embarrassing) but I still did it because I wanted to communicate. Cindy rolled her eyes, but she loved it. One year, I wrote her a letter every day. We still have these letters. If things get tough, I can read them to myself and remind myself of how much I love her. Most relationships start out with that sort of stuff, but fast forward a couple months or years and we find ourselves not communicating as effectively as we did back when we were dating. What took place? What happened? Why did we stop being effective communicators?"

Here's why: Somewhere along the line a subtle and hideous shift takes place. We start communicating not to become *one*, but to *win*.

This is not complicated. We enter negotiations and conflict because we want it our way rather than God's way.

> The first way we try to win is through negotiation.
> When negotiation fails, we try to win through conflict.

Negotiation is creating margins within the Word of God where what God's Word says really isn't that important. And we become a negotiator with our husband, our groom, Jesus Christ. Guess what? When you begin to negotiate the Word of God, and your relationship with your groom, Jesus, you'll begin to negotiate with your spouse, and there become margins. But when you become a communicator, and communication takes place, you are not negotiating. It says it, you do it. You say it, you do it. And that's what great communication does. Don't negotiate... communicate. Share clear expectation, and you will avoid negotiation.

When negotiations fail and conflict breaks out, forget about trying to figure out a solution that might work for everybody. It's all or nothing—winner takes all at any cost.

But if just one spouse wins, both lose—because God designed us to be one. Great communication isn't about getting our way; it's about doing it God's way.

> And this is my prayer: that your love may abound more and more in knowledge and depth of insight, so that you may be able to discern what is best and may be pure and blameless for the day of Christ, filled with the fruit of righteousness that comes through Jesus Christ—to the glory and praise of God.—Philippians 1:9-11

What a powerful prayer! Paul looks at the leg of love under the table of marriage and he wants it to "abound more and more." Who wouldn't want that!? Now notice that love abounds "in knowledge and depth of insight". Key phrases there. Knowledge and insight can come through awesome communication, so you can "discern what is best and may be pure."

The table of marriage simply cannot stand without the legs of love and forgiveness. It's this third leg, communication, however, that makes it sTABLE—enduring, permanent, not likely to fall or give way.

That's communication, and you guessed it, it happens at the table.

BREAKING THE NEGOTIATION/CONFLICT CYCLE

The most important communication skill is as profound as it is simple. But it takes discernment, wisdom, and the willingness to let the spirit of God reveal, and then apply it. Researchers and therapists pontificate about this unequivocally profound technique for breaking the negotiation/conflict cycle. What is it? Shut up. That's it. Know when to close your trap and you can derail that vast majority destructive communication.

How do you know when to put a cork in it? Answering "Yes" to any one of the following four questions means it's time to H.A.L.T. the conversation:

H-"Am I hungry?" HALT!
A -"Am I angry?" HALT!
L- "Am I lonely?" HALT!
T- "Am I tired?" HALT!

Hungry?

Trying to communicate when hungry can easily start the negotiation/conflict cycle. It can also lead to some really stupid decisions. Esau is a classic example of how communication can go really bad at the table. Esau came home from day of hunting and he was starving. Check out the dialog in (passage). Seriously, he sounded a lot like me when I'm hungry. He was gruff, impatient, demanding, and extremely shortsighted. Because of his hunger, he entered into negotiations with his brother, Jacob, and actually gave up the inheritance of his birthright for a bowl of soup! If he would've recognized that he was hungry and that he needed to

H.A.L.T. the conversation, he would've been a lot better off and would have broken the negotiation/conflict cycle immediately.

Magic phrases:

- "Honey, I'm famished. Let's talk about this after I've had some chow."
- "I understand this is important. Let's talk about this at the table... a table with food on it!"

Angry?

> Therefore each of you must put off falsehood and speak truthfully to your neighbor, for we are all members of one body. "In your anger do not sin": Do not let the sun go down while you are still angry, and do not give the devil a foothold.—Ephesians 4:25-27

In our fallen world full of sin, anger is a part of life. It's possible to be angry and not sin, and forgiveness defuses anger before it has a chance to really explode. Anger needs to be dealt with. When Paul says "Don't let the sun go down while you are still angry", I don't think he means that literally. If you get angry early evening, you don't have to figure it out before sunset in five minutes. If you get ticked off just after dusk, that doesn't mean you have 24 hours to run around with steam pouring out of your ears. He's saying deal with it *soon*. You can be angry and not sin; but staying angry leads to an awful lot of sin.

> Do not let your mouth lead you into sin. –Ecclesiastes 5:6

> An angry person stirs up conflict, and a hot-tempered person commits many sins.—Proverbs 29:22

It's not unbiblical to argue with your mate as long as you are sincerely working toward oneness. I will go one step further and say, don't waste a good argument. Learn and grow from it. Anger, however, can launch you into negotiation, and conflict, where all you ever do is argue. That's different. It may be because you're unwilling to relinquish your pride and truly come to a biblical resolution that creates a marital resolve. If neither one of you are willing to submit to God and each other it's going to be a mess. So when you realize you are angry, H.A.L.T., back off and shut up.

Magic phrases:

- "My attitude stinks right now and it's getting worse. Give me a while to cool down."
- "Let's take a break so I can take a deep breath. Can we sit down at the table tonight with a cup of coffee?
- "I can tell you are frustrated right now. Let's call a time out and come back to this

If this doesn't help you break the cycle, or if your anger *ever* becomes physical or emotionally abusive, get help before you hurt anyone further. Period.

Lonely?

It's really hard to communicate when you feel disconnected. When negotiations fail and the conflict has worn you out, you might feel really alone. That is not a good time to try to talk *until* you take it to Christ and have some real table-time with him.

> Marriage should be honored by all, and the marriage bed kept pure, for God will judge the adulterer and all the sexually immoral. Keep your lives free from the love of money and be content with what you have, because God has said, "Never will I leave you; never will I forsake you."—Hebrews 13:4-5

See the connection? How many affairs would have been avoided, how many arguments about money could have been dodged if we had just chosen to H.A.L.T. and spend some time restoring our connection with God who has promised to never leave us or forsake us?

Loneliness is tough… it sucks the life out of you. When you're not getting oneness with your spouse, be sure you are getting it from your Lord. Then you can come back to the marriage table with a full tank of love and start communicating in a way that leads toward oneness rather than negotiation and conflict.

Magic phrases:

- "Hey, I'm kind of hurting right now. I'm going spend some time with the Lord and then we can pick up this conversation after that."
- "I can tell you're feeling alone, isolated and unappreciated right now. Why don't we go get naked or go for a walk in the park (or whatever speaks love to your mate) and then pray about this?"

Tired?

I don't need to explain this one, do I? You know what happens to you when you haven't had enough sleep. Recognize it and H.A.L.T. communication before you tip over into negotiation and conflict.

Magic phrases:

- "Honey, I'm bushed. Let me sleep on it and we will talk about it over breakfast."
- "I can tell you are worn out. No need to figure this out right now. I'll take care of the kids, you take a nap and then we can talk about it."

TWO EARS, ONE MOUTH

Remember Paul's prayer *"that your love may abound more and more in knowledge and depth of insight?"* That only happens when somebody listens. Awesome communication becomes possible when you shut up. It *begins* when you listen—and I mean *really* listen. I'm not talking about nodding your head while formulating your next comeback in your mind while the other person talks. I'm talking about *active* listening that seeks knowledge and insight from the *other* person by asking good questions. Active listening:

- Buys you time to get your head together and your heart in the right place.
- Helps you understand what's going on so you can eventually respond in wisdom.
- Affirms the others importance by making them feel understood and loved.
- Leads to good decisions.

Magic Phrases:

- "I'm not sure I understand. Can you explain that in a different way?"
- "So, what you are saying is___. Do I have it right?".
- "Do you feel like I've heard you out?"

SPEAKING TRUTH IN LOVE

After you have shut up and really listened, *then* it's your turn to talk. The Bible is filled with powerful principles for communicating in a way that leads to oneness rather than negotiation and conflict.

> [29] Do not let any unwholesome talk come out of your mouths, but only what is helpful for building others up according to their needs, that it may benefit those who listen...[31] Get rid of all bitterness, rage and anger, brawling and slander, along with every form of malice. [32] Be kind and compassionate to one another, forgiving each other, just as in Christ God forgave you.—Ephesians 4:29-32

Notice how this passage ties communication leg of the marriage table into the love and forgiveness legs. Here's a couple ways to get started:

1. Express appreciation.

Some of you spent a bunch of jack to pay for the wedding of your dreams. Some of you sailed a lot of miles to get that dad convinced that she was meant to be with you. Why would you not share appreciation? You might have some hard things to say later, but start the conversation with something that you genuinely and positively feel.

2. Take responsibility for your conflict.

I'm talking about more than just confessing your sin and asking for forgiveness (although that's certainly part of this). I'm talking about accepting the fact that God has created you to be one flesh. You're in war. It's not easy. It's tough. We have jobs. We have stuff going on but the two of you are one. Take ownership and responsibility for both of you. You're the same person. If you would transition that mentally everything would change in your marriage. Maybe you're not there yet? Does this level of oneness seem impossible? Hang in there. As love, forgiveness and communication become a reality, this type of oneness will be the fruit.

3. Share your criticism and complaining in a problem-solving context.

Don't just come blowing in the door, hot. When you want to enter negotiations or conflict, take those critical moments and look for an opportunity to make them constructive and centered around God's best. Jesus regularly encouraged and spurred one another on to love and good deeds, especially with the disciples. His Spirit lives in you, and can do the same through you.

> I can do all this through him who gives me strength."— Philippians 4:13

Conflict and negotiation cycles WILL happen, but you can break them with love, forgiveness and good communication. In it doesn't mean problems go way. It means you can deal with them in a way that creates oneness rather than division. Trust me, Cindy and I have been there.

Just a year or two into our marriage I pulled off a doozie. We should have H.A.L.T.ed, because I was getting angry and neither of us was actively listening at all. Finally, I let it fly. "If you wanted your husband to be like your dad, you should have married him!" It took a couple days for her to come around. I asked her forgiveness immediately, but it took her a while. It took a while before she could release this. But we lived to fight another day.

One of those days came a couple years ago. There was a person our church who had really been hurting me. I felt like he was ripping my guts out and dumping a truckload of salt over everything. Then one night Cindy and I tipped over into the conflict cycle and she pulled out the big guns. "Now I know why Bill is always so mad at you! Now I know why he hates you!" That was the worst, and most damaging phrase that I had ever heard in my life. She used my enemy to give herself approval of why she should hate me too? Oh man. It tore me up. I walked away certain that our relationship could never be repaired.

But before the sun went down, she came to me and asked my forgiveness. By God's grace I was able to forgive her. She was in tears and broken over it, but it was one of those moments where you think "that's it, we're done". But we weren't done. And you aren't done either. God is in this with you and your spouse and the three of you can find a better way.

> Because of the LORD's great love we are not consumed, for his compassions never fail. They are new every morning; great is your faithfulness. I say to myself, "The LORD is my portion; therefore I will wait for him."—Lamentations 3:22-24

SWITCHING IT UP

Somebody once defined "insanity" as "doing the same thing over and over and expecting a different result."

Are *you* insane?

I'm throwing some good stuff at you. But nothing is going to change if you keep doing the same thing over and over. You don't have to worry about going back into the cycle of rejection and conflict. If you don't switch it up, you're going to *stay* in that cycle. If you keep saying, "Man, I'm just not a good communicator," you might as well call it quits. It's probably better to be hopeless than insane!

Do you believe that you are created in God's image? Scripture says you are. Do you believe the Spirit of God lives in you? Scripture says he does. Don't diss the way that he has created you. Don't diss what he has put in you. Things can change if you trust in him and are willing to do things differently.

Doing it differently will feel uncomfortable, awkward and maybe even silly at first. But are you willing to quit doing the same thing over and over so that you can get a different result? Are you willing to switch it up so *"that your love may abound more and more in knowledge and depth of insight?"* If so, I've got some ideas.

1. **Use the table.** Tables are ideal places to develop new patterns of communication. Jesus was passionate about the table and he used it as a strategic place to connect with all sorts of different people. When you see a table, think about change. Think about how you can use that flat, four-legged piece of furniture to break the cycle and be one.

2. **Use a recorder.** The other day Cindy and I were really in a heated argument and I was pretty sure we were going to forget what we were saying. So I just snuck my smart phone from my pocket, turned on an app called Voice Recorder, hit "record" and sat my phone down. Sure enough, Cindy started to get confused.

"No, that's *not* what you said," she said. "Yes, that *is* what I said," I said. "No, it's not." "Yes, it is". After we repeated those two phrases about 9,251 times, I stopped, smiled deviously and said, "Really?"

When I showed her that I'd been recording, she pushed back from the table in obvious defeat. But guess what, I was totally busted. She had it right, I had it wrong. Yeah, I had to adjust my attitude a little bit there, but I was actually glad. When you want to *win* truth doesn't even matter. But when you want to be *one,* love and truth is at the center. I hated proving myself wrong, but right there the spirit broke the cycle of negotiation and conflict. Now, we use that recorder when things get hot. I mean, not like *hot-hot* (there's other apps for that will talk about in the next chapter!) I mean "heated". It works for us. Mix it up and try recording yourselves.

3. **Write it out.** About a month ago, Cindy was trying to tell me about five major issues in our relationship there were urgent. They weren't eternal necessarily, but they were immediate, and I just wasn't listening. So she did something so brilliant. She typed out the five things she was trying to say in an email. I received that email and through that piece of communication I was able to see so clearly exactly what she was trying to say. I let it soak in for about thirty minutes, took a breath, called her and said, "You're exactly right, I'm an idiot." And that part was really true, I can promise you that. By switching to writing, Cindy helped me to shut up and listen. I had to ask myself, "Was I really arguing over these five things?"

4. **Find a solid mediator/counselor.** Satan is a liar. I think one of his most effective lies is convincing Christians that they're supposed to have their act together. That turns *us* into liars. We run around faking everything, pretending that we're strong and independent. It's better to be honest, genuine and transparent. I'm not saying you throw all your marriage junk out there on Main Street, but you do need to be honest with somebody safe. For Cindy and me that somebody is Dr. Jonathan Cude, a licensed Christian counselor in Dallas. There is a table in his office, and when he sits us down at the table, we know it's time for business. It can get uncomfortable at that table, but it's a safe place where we get help.

I don't care that some people might think that means we are weak. I *am* weak. We are *all* weak in *all* sorts of ways. Everybody gets professional advice from doctors, professors, lawyers, realtors and mechanics etc. Only pride, and Satan's lie, keeps us from seeking counsel in the most important area of our lives: relationships. But I'm talking about healthy biblically-based intervention. I'm not talking about some soft-serve, tell-me-what-I-want-to-hear, feel good stuff. We pay good money to get solid, godly counsel. And it's worth every penny, because our marriage is worth it.

So is yours.

Every marriage is worth the investment of good communication. God has revealed how and he is waiting to switch things up for you and your spouse if you will just let him.

Dear God,

I ask that my marriage would abound more and more in love through knowledge and insight. Convict me about my role in the negotiation/conflict cycle. In the name of Jesus, by the power of the Spirit in me, I believe that I am a great communicator. Make me willing to H.A.L.T. when I need to. Give me a listening heart. Speak the truth through me in love.

Amen.

AT THE TABLE WITH JESUS

Great communication with your spouse starts with great communication with your Creator, and both can get a jump start at the table. Because of the cross, a personal relationship with God is possible through Christ and the Holy Spirit, and the same principles of communication apply!

1. Get alone with the Lord at a table. And then just shut up for a while. Give your brain a rest even if just for a few minutes.

Ask God to clear your thoughts so you can really hear what he wants to say to you.

2. Listen to what God is saying to you in Ephesians 4. Read and ponder the whole chapter a couple of times. Write a note back to him restating what you sense he is telling you.

3. Talk with him about what is on your heart. Ask him to break the cycles of negotiation and conflict in your marriage and to build a new level of oneness where your love abounds more and more in knowledge and insight.

4. Follow his lead as he points you to new and different things he wants you to do in your communication.

5. Give those things to the Lord and trust that he will do it through you in his strength. You can do all things through Christ who strengthens you!

AT THE TABLE WITH YOUR SPOUSE

Plan on mixing it up! We are all about breaking cycles and doing things different, so go to a table somewhere you have never been before as a couple—Maybe at a campground, or a zoo or an amusement park.

1. Rehearse the H.A.L.T. by sharing how Hunger, Anger, Loneliness and Tiredness affect your communication. Pick out a couple of the "magic phrases" that you think will be appropriate when the two of you stand on the edge of the negotiation/conflict cycle. You might want to write down a few phrases of your own. Practice saying those phrases to each other SEVERAL TIMES. Make a commitment to respect the other person's wishes when they call for a "time out".

2. Read Philippians 1:1-11 together. Highlight or underline the phrases that are most important to you a couple. What is God trying to say to you?

3. Brainstorm on new ways the two of you can communicate. What do you think about using recordings? What if you started

writing letters and notes? How could you use social media? Pick one new way to start with and give it a try!

4. Discuss where you can find a good mediator or counselor. What would be some of the advantages to connecting with someone like that at the table?

5. Hold hands and pray (silently or out-loud) through Philippians 1:9-11. Make it *your* prayer for *your* marriage.

FOR GROUP DISCUSSION

1. In your opinion, rank the importance of the four legs on the table of marriage.

   Love Forgiveness Communication Sex

   Could the table stand without one or more of these legs? Why or why not?

2. Do you think that every divorce or affair happens because of the negotiation/conflict cycle?

   If someone disagreed with your answer, what might they use as evidence?

3. Do you think good communication can guarantee that a divorce or affair won't happen? Why do you think that?

4. Brainstorm on different and creative ways to communicate love and appreciation. Do you think these are universal to all people in all situations? Support you answer with examples.

Table 1: Marriage

Leg #4: Red Hot Sex

> The LORD God said, "It is not good for the man to be alone…
> That is why a man leaves his father and mother and is united to
> his wife, and they become one flesh. Adam and his wife were
> both naked, and they felt no shame.
>
> —Genesis 2:18, 24-25

igniTABLE [ig-nit-*uh*-bu*h*l] *adjective*
1. to set something on fire.
2. to give life or energy to someone.

I love my job almost all the time. There are weeks where I definitely earn my paycheck, but for the most part, I get paid to have a front-row seat to watch God change lives.

The most amazing things I get to see first -hand, one of my favorites is seeing marriages catch fire at our "Romance Uncensored" events and conferences. It's really a shame what has happened to sex. I'm not talking about sex on the Internet, on the streets, or in the entertainment industry; I'm talking about sex in Christianity. For some reason, sex has gotten majorly censored in the church. Nobody really talks about it unless it's all negative or unless it's the junk we are all supposed to *not* do: *don't have an affair, don't look at pornography, don't have sex before marriage, and don't lust*—then we are living in God's will, right? Not in my mind. The church has done a great job teaching purity and a poor job at teaching marital passion. Sex is worship. God created it, so we can participate in intimate worship with our spouse.

In the beginning, God created us male and female. He designed us for oneness in *every* way. Yes, that includes emotional and spiritual stuff, but come on! The most obvious part of his design for oneness is physical. The male and female body was created to be smooshed together in a hormone-injected, turbo-passionate, ultra-intense embrace. "Naked and unashamed" all wrapped up together until you can't tell where one person ends an the other one starts so they become "one flesh."

That's the biblical design, but when Adam and Eve turned from God's perfect plan back in the Garden of Eden, their immediate response was to hide themselves from each other with clothing, and then to hide from God himself. Suddenly, when they deviated from his plan, their sexuality became taboo and shameful. We have been censoring the topic of sex ever since. Worst of all, because of Satan's lies, created we've created a mental, emotional and spiritual barrier between sex and God—and it's robbing us. Instead sex being worship in marriage, we worship sex outside of marriage. I know life is never going be perfect like it was in the garden. But I say it's time to tell Satan to go to hell, and to begin to reclaim and pursue the sexual heaven that God created us to experience on this Earth. I say it's time to *un*-censor romance and talk openly and boldly about God, sexuality, and the Scriptures.

The table of marriage stands on love, forgiveness and communication *and* full-on, hot, erotic, out of the box sexual intimacy. I know it might sound strange and awkward to hear those kinds of words coming from a "Christian" book. But I can't be fully Christian without fully embracing *everything* that God says, and He says a lot about sex... and some of it even happens at the table! That's what I call being "compaTABLE," because sex, God and the table of marriage can all work together when you glorify God with your bodies as he intends.

THE GOD/SEX BARRIER

If there is any question in your mind that God intended sex to be free, frequent pleasurable and highly erotic, look no further than the Bible. The Song of Solomon is devoted almost entirely to sex. Some theologians have tried to explain it away as being "a literary metaphor for God's love for the church." Honestly, I see a few verses in that book that *could* be interpreted that way, but gimme a break: This book of the Bible is a steamy hot love letter. The whole first chapter is clearly about sexual foreplay. And where does it happen? You guessed it. At the table. Can it happen? It's inevitable.

² Let him kiss me with the kisses of his mouth— for your love is more delightful than wine…4 Take me away with you—let us hurry! Let the king bring me into his chambers…

¹² **While the king was at his table, my perfume spread its fragrance.**

¹³ My beloved is to me a sachet of myrrh resting between my breasts.

¹⁴ My beloved is to me a cluster of henna blossoms from the vineyards of En Gedi. —Song of Solomon 1:2, 4, 12-14

I don't know what a sachet of myrrh or a henna blossom is and I've never been to the vineyards of En Gedi, but if Cindy is into it, I'd love to find out some night… you know, just to follow what the Bible says! It's tastefully written, but this is X-rated stuff. One chapter later, Solomon's bride even describes the two of them in a heavy petting situation and warns other women not to go there until they're ready, because they probably won't be able to stop.

> His left arm is under my head,
> and his right arm embraces me.
> ⁷ Daughters of Jerusalem, I charge you
> by the gazelles and by the does of the field:
> Do not arouse or awaken love
> until it so desires. —Song of Solomon 2:6-7

I could go further, but in all honesty, my publisher wouldn't carry this book if I get as explicit as the Bible does. Notice that the whole encounter begins loving words of affirmation adoration and affection. Notice that she perfumes him while he's "at the table." There's tons of practical and advice in here. No joke, you get a couple paragraphs into this book and you're either going to need a cold shower you're going to need to find your spouse *fast*. This is kindling, and fuel, for burning hot passion between a husband and a wife. Song of Solomon even talks about how to create an irresistible erotic environment. It includes some crazy anatomical descriptions for sexual body parts, and it does so without any shame... But I'm getting ahead of myself. The point I'm trying to make is simply this:

Our holy God wanted a steamy hot love letter in the Holy Scriptures because a red-hot sexual marriage *is* holy.

Seriously, who do you think invented sex in the first place?

> [18] The LORD God said, "It is not good for the man to be alone... So the LORD God caused the man to fall into a deep sleep; and while he was sleeping, he took one of the man's ribs and then closed up the place with flesh. [22] Then the LORD God made a woman from the rib he had taken out of the man, and he brought her to the man.

> [23] The man said, "This is now bone of my bones and flesh of my flesh; she shall be called 'woman,' for she was taken out of man." [24] That is why a man leaves his father and mother and is united to his wife, and they become one flesh. [25] Adam and his wife were both naked, and they felt no shame. —Genesis 2:18, 23-25

One flesh, naked and no shame, that's God's design. (Jesus even quoted this passage in Matthew 19 and Mark 10. Paul quoted it in 1 Corinthians 6 and Ephesians 5.) That deserves more than a head nod or a golf clap. That deserves a full-on hallelujah stand up jump up-and-down praise the Lord. I'm telling you, if you want to get into sex, get into God's Word, the way he designed it.

> May your fountain be blessed, and may you rejoice in the wife of your youth. A loving doe, a graceful deer—may her breasts satisfy you always, may you ever be intoxicated with her love. —Proverbs 5:18-19

If you look at the verses around this one, God is openly talking about boobs, semen and pheromones—And he's saying we should get drunk with it. Bring it on! What breaks my heart is how many couples operate in an institution that God created (marriage) without even having God involved. It's really foolish to think that we would be a part of a institution and never ask the designer's opinion or investigate what he says about it.

God designed each of the legs of the table of marriage (Love, forgiveness, communication and sex) so that a husband and wife could be one in every way. I love my marriage when I can just look at my wife from 100 yards off and already know everything she is thinking and what I need to do about it, positive or negative. If we don't embrace the sexual as sacred, you are going to think it is forbidden, and how you think about sex is the kind of sex you're going to have. If you think stolen sex is good, you're gonna be addicted to porn, be tempted to find release from someone besides your spouse, probably get addicted to someone else's emotion and set yourself up for divorce.

CONNECTING THE SEXUAL WITH THE SACRED AT THE TABLE

One of the best anniversary gifts Cindy has given me was a bedroom makeover. She bought a bunch of battery powered candles and little trees with lights all over them. Then she had a friend come over and repainted the entire bedroom. To top it off, she stenciled this beautiful phrase on our back wall: "With you I am complete…With you I have everything."

She changed it all, creating a godly space where we can celebrate being one flesh. Is your bedroom like that? Go to your bedroom mentally right now and look at it. What do you see in your mind? How does it make you feel?

Take some advice from Solomon and create surroundings that are blistering, beautiful and hot. Let's start by clearing some stuff out of the way:

- The computer.
- The crib.
- The mail.
- The laundry.
- The desk.

You need to get that stuff out of there. You've got better things to do in that space. The bedroom is not the place for Facebook or business or news or chores. God says the marriage bed should stay *pure*. So clear out the junk and replace it with things that can transform that room into a place where the sacred and the sexual come together like God intended.

It's not just a bedroom; it's a sanctuary, a cathedral and a chapel. Why? Because sex is *worship*.

Sorry, did I just enter the weird zone? Well, think about it!

> Do you not know that your body is a temple of the Holy Spirit who is in you, whom you have from God, and that you are not your own?
>
> —1 Corinthians 6:19

> Therefore I urge you, brethren, by the mercies of God, to present your bodies a living and holy sacrifice, acceptable to God, which is your spiritual service of worship. —Romans 12:1

> Marriage should be honored by all, and the marriage bed kept pure...
>
> —Heb 13:4

God isn't just into sex as the one who created it and designed it. He is actually into you. If you've asked him into your life, his Spirit resides in your spirit making your fleshly body a temple of worship.

This whole division that we have created in our minds between the sacred and the sexual is just flat out wrong. So I'm going to suggest replacing the junk in your bedroom with a table that can help you change your mind about that: the bedside table. You might already have one, and it's probably cluttered with a bunch of junk. If you don't have one, buy one of those little wooden ones and lay a nice piece of cloth over it. Then, as a couple, place a few things on it that will remind you that your bedroom is a sacred place of intimate worship for you and your spouse:

- Candles
- Oil (often used in the Bible for anointing and healing)
- Incense
- Love letters
- Speakers and an iPhone full of "worship" music.
- A lock on the drawer so your kids don't take this stuff out and show it to their friends.

Most importantly, remove all insecurities, become vulnerable, with no separation between the sacred and the sexual when you come together as God intended.

Jesus did this for you. He did on the cross for you, naked and unashamed He gave His life for you. Now with hearts full of worship and praise, give yourself unashamed to your spouse.

BREAKING THROUGH

When Adam and Eve chose to do things their own way, a lot of things got messed up. Getting things right with God and realizing the sacredness of sex is a huge step in rediscovering his original design for intimacy on all levels. But that doesn't mean that all sexual struggles are going to magically disappear. We must understand that sex is a mandate in a healthy Christ centered marriage.

> Do not deprive each other except perhaps by mutual consent and for a time, so that you may devote yourselves to prayer. Then come together again so that Satan will not tempt you because of your lack of self-control. —1 Corinthians 7:5

Here are few remedies that will help your struggles, and your spouses sexual needs.

Physical/Medical Challenges

Sex is definitely a physical act, and when our human physique isn't functioning perfectly, it can be a barrier to sex.

I'm not a medical physician, but I will say this, medications can change you. They can make it difficult to have an erection or kill a woman's emotional sexual desires. Take a look at your hormone medication. Reconsider your depression medications. Get a second opinion. Find out if you really need it. Some of that really messes up you sex life.

It's no surprise that age take a toll on your physical body as well. Between the ages of 40 and 55, women go through "menopause" (I call it men-on-pause) and some men go through "andropause" when hormones shift and sexual drive and stamina can change. If you suspect a physical cause, talk to a qualified professional. Often times they can help. Certain medications are making of vibrant sex life possible decades longer than before.

In some cases, physical problems make intercourse impossible. But that doesn't mean your sex life dies. There are tons of ways that you can experience orgasm without having intercourse. There are so many ways that you can pleasure each other and share physical intimacy "until death do you part," regardless of physical limitations. If you've got challenges, talk about it, first with your spouse and then someone who can help.

Getting out of Shape

My wife told me recently, "Shannon, I think you are made for Crossfit." (In the greek that translates, "You need to lose weight.") I told her I would pray about it, and I committed to 90 days, and now have been at my box for over a year. She was right, I do love everything about Crossfit, and the blessing it has been to my marriage.

When your body is out of shape, your sex life can whither. It's all about the blood flow. If you don't keep your heart pumping like it should, your sexual stamina at can suffer. But getting in shape is also great for your mind and your communication. Start exercising and eating right as a couple. And if you need a new incentive to do a workout video, try it together with the door locked and the lights down low. You never know what might happen.

The Uglies

Appearance isn't everything, but it is something. Even in a good marriage, it's easy to get lackadaisical with things that can throw a damper on our sex life. A couple suggestions:

Guys, the gold and blue band whitie-tighties need to go. There ain't nobody that needs to be wearing that underwear to bed. Ladies, it's time to burn the grannie-panties. You know what I'm talking about. Your mom wore them and so did her mom's mom. Time to break the chain and find something silky and smooth. You are worth it and he will appreciate it. And if anything either of you wear has stains in 'em, throw 'em in the trash! You're laughing but you know it's real.

A shave, shower and a little bit of cologne or perfume can make a big difference. I know there's plenty of things that you can't change, but your mate will appreciate it if you change the things you can do make a difference to them. Guys, if she doesn't like the hair on your back, Nair works—but don't use that stuff on your privates. I had a friend who went on a cruise and Nair'd some inappropriate areas. He never saw the ocean. Five days in the infirmary!

Emotional/material adultery

The heart and mind are indispensable sex organs. If either of those is in the wrong place, your sex life at home won't be in the right place. You know what I'm talking about. Particularly when a marriage has cooled off or is going through tough times, it is so tempting to seek emotional intimacy somewhere else.

That's why, men, you have to guard where your wife works, if she does work. I'm not saying you should be some crazy man with a shotgun all the time—a lot of the time, yes. Okay, so you need to be that way *all* the time. You need to protect her guys, because you know how we can be. There is no greater intimacy than her knowing you're protecting her from working in a tempting environment where some dude is playing to her emotional needs. You need to check where your affections are as well. Does your wife have to work in some place where some guy will be hitting on her every day so that she can bring in an extra $20,000 a year so you can make an extra payment on cable TV, the car you want, or a hunting lease? I'm just calling it like it is, okay? It's the same trap for both genders. Wanting more stuff means more work and more temptation that can kill your sex life and your marriage. It's crazy, but advertisers are spending billions to convince you that if you buy their stuff, sex comes with it: Beer, cars, clothes, perfume—you name it. They try to sell it all with the promise of sex. But isn't all that junk a *distraction* from good sex as God designed it? Forget the stuff. Go for the priceless things.

The Dreaded Yawn

Variety is the spice of life, and even too much of a good thing can become, well, boring. Sex was not designed to be boring. Do you know who I serve? I serve a God who is creative. He has created all kinds of tingly and sensitive stuff that is so much fun and somebody needs to learn more about it. Amen?

After two decades of marriage, I thought maybe we tried everything. But Cindy and I had one of the best dates of our lives just a couple of weeks ago. We got on four-wheeler and went exploring. I'm not going to say exactly what we explored or how we were sitting on the four wheeler, but I can tell that I can drive one of those things sitting backwards. That's all I'm saying about that, but what I'm really saying is that a little creativity destroys boredom. New music, new positions, new places, new schedules… as long as you are both into it, go for it.

What other things does your mate like? Maybe you could mix it up with that? Knitting? ar racing? Romantic chick-flicks? Football playoffs? Think about it then shock them with *your* thoughtful creativity.

Just look around. What could you do with a can of whipped cream or a cake sprinkles? As long as we are talking about tables, what could happen *at* one, *on* one or *under* one? I dare you!

No Sex? No Talk.
No Talk? No Sex.

The number one complaint that Cindy and I hear from women is that their husbands don't talk very much. The first question I always ask them is this, "How often do you give him hot sex?" They don't seem to see the connection.

What's the number one complaint from men? "My wife doesn't want to have sex very much." The first question I always ask them is this, "How often do you really communicate your love to her?" Guys, here's a great way to start your night of sex: Start by by clamming up acting all neglected. Then say, "Haven't had any in three days." Oh, I can promise you you're definitely, definitely going to get laid that night. Laid out!

Listen, I don't think there's anything that launches a marriage into the negotiating/conflict cycle like sex and communication. One definitely leads to the other.

The question is this: What really comes first, good sex or good communication?

Sexual intimacy creates great communication. Communication intimacy creates great sex. And *either* partner can make the first move when they allow the love of Christ to move through them. In love, both partners *should* make the first move on a regular basis.

In the ideal situation, both partners are trusting in Christ to love the other person through them, and forgiving the other person when they don't live up to their expectations. If both of you are initiating good communication, and setting the stage for great sex, the negotiation/conflict cycle won't even get started. If both of you get selfish and start withholding love from your mate, it's a disaster in the making.

You need to create a level of intimacy expectation:

- Call, text, maybe even Snapchat each other throughout the day.
- Buy a new piece of lingerie, or flowers, and sneak them into your mate's purse or briefcase.

- Dump the kids for the evening and go out to dinner or have just a special dinner alone at home.
- Find a new and clear way to share your desires and expectations.
- Get cleaned up and dress for the occasion.
- Write notes to each other.
- Etc. etc. etc....

The possibilities are endless. Do anything and everything to create healthy communication and sexual expectation. And your love will take care of the rest.

RED HOT

If you're willing to do what it takes to break through the barriers to awesome sexual intimacy, your marriage can become red-hot. And you know what? The world doesn't know what to do with a marriage that is red hot. I wear this shirt all of the time that says, "My wife is hot." No one knows what to do with that shirt, nobody! They're like, "Did she buy that for ya? Hahahaha!" "No," I tell them. "I paid for it myself. Matter of fact, I made it." And they're like, "Oh." There is a lady that I had never met that read my shirt. She had a big grin, and then she got kind of sad and said, "I wonder if my husband would wear a shirt like that..." That made me sad too.

I'm not suggesting everybody gets a shirt like that. If you do, I'll need to come up with something else to let Cindy know my love for her is unique and intense. So come up with some stuff of your own, okay? And if your sex life needs a tune up, or if it's broke and you don't know how to fix it, I'm telling you to get help from the right place. Everybody needs it. Cindy and I get it all the time. And it's available to anyone.

Marriage retreats are a great place to start. Most churches have then. Other organizations offer them. Most mediators and counselors are used to helping couples with sex. If you sit across the table from an expert (and someone who is well grounded in the Word) huge problems can often be resolved easily. One couple came into a counseling center with really significant negotiation/conflict issues. They dug down through a decade of issues, but at the bottom, the counselor discovered that the wife had never had an orgasm. She felt continually used in bed and deeply resented it. They were a "good Christian" couple and had never talked to anyone about it. The counselor explained just a few details of female anatomy and WOW! It broke the negotiation/conflict cycle and lit the fire for a red hot marriage.

All four legs of the table are necessary. When one is broken it affects all the others. But when all four are in place? Love, forgiveness, healthy communication *and* hot, regular sex make the table of marriage rock solid, and all four legs make the table of marriage a powerful place to display the love of Christ to the world.

ALONE AT THE TABLE WITH JESUS

Christ has promised that he will always be with you and that he will never leave you. God knows your thoughts, He knows your desires… He just knows! It's time to get along with him and finally get completely real with him about sex. You can't tell him anything that he doesn't know. You don't have any desires or frustrations that he is not aware of. And there's a good chance that you've let the lies of Satan and the results of the fall compartmentalize your sexuality from the sacredness of God.

Ponder:

- Spend some time meditating on Song of Solomon. Imagine that he is describing you and your spouse.

Pour out your heart:

- Ask the Holy Spirit to search your heart and to reveal areas and issues of your sexuality that you have never openly communicated to God.
- You might need to confess some things that nobody else knows about. Whatever it is that's on your heart, talk to him about

it. He will never forsake you nor will he ever reject you. His forgiveness flows to every area of your life.

- You may have frustrations that you've been embarrassed to tell him about. Tell him everything right now. He knows anyway!
- You may have never asked him to be the central focus of your sexual relationship with your spouse. Talk to him about that.

Listen:
- From what you have read in His Word and what he is revealing to your spirit, what is he telling you about sex and worship?
- What else is he speaking to you? Talk to him about it!

AT THE TABLE WITH YOUR SPOUSE

First, find a table in a fairly public place, but somewhere you can talk openly with each other.

- Go back through this chapter and talk about whatever seems to be most important to each of you.
- Share anything important from your personal time at the table with Jesus.
- What would be the advantages of going to a marriage conference or retreat?
- What would it be like to go through one of the resources listed at the end of this chapter?
- Are there any stubborn issues that you think could be helped by a mediator or a counselor?
- Reread the section about transforming your bedroom into a place of worship and preparing a bedside table. What particular things do you want on your table to symbolize the sacredness of your sexuality?

Next, work together to buy anything you want to transform your bedroom and prepare your table together. Get ready to do it right! Light the candles, turn on the music and wear your favorites.

Together, kneeling at that table you have prepared, read your favorite passage from the Song of Solomon,

Then make some new vows to each other!

Husband:

"I commit my body to you free of shame, wholly yours, taking care of my temple for your utmost pleasure as worship to our God, in the name of the Father, in the name of the Son, in the name of the Holy Spirit.:

Wife:

"I was created for you, sexually, to meet your needs and to be your joy. I commit now to pleasure you and no one else for the rest of our lives. Take me now, I'm yours. In the name of the Father, the son and the Holy Spirit."

FOR GROUP DISCUSSION

- How is the topic of sex treated in your church? Do you think it is healthy or unhealthy?
- Give examples to support your opinion.
- Read Genesis 2. Look for insights into how sin affected Adam and Eve's sexuality.
- Why do you think sex taboo in most Christian circles?
- Can you give historical, spiritual and cultural reasons?
- What could you, as a group, do to "un-censor" the topic of sex?

TABLE 2: PARENTING

Leg #1: Love

See what great love the Father has lavished on us, that we should be called children of God! And that is what we are!... ² Dear friends, now we are children of God, and what we will be has not yet been made known. But we know that when Christ appears, we shall be like him, for we shall see him as he is.

—1 John 3:1-2

exciTABLE [ik-sahy-t*uh*-b*uh*l] *adjective*
1. Capable of being awakened aroused or stirred up to action.
2. The ignition in a child's soul when they experience love at the table.

THERE ARE FEW things more intimate than eating dinner with people you value, honor and desire... and there is no one I value, honor and desire more than my family. Sometimes, when we're at the table, I just sit back in my chair and soak it all in. I wish I could take a 3-D photograph and just freeze frame some of the moments that we have together at the table. I love hearing my children laugh and tell stories and say, "Mom, that is the best I've ever had!" I love talking about our days and what they learned at school, and holding hands and giving thanks for all He has done... Man, I'm telling you, these are busy, chaotic years in our house, but when everybody is seated around the table face-to-face, everything in the world just seems right, even if for just a few minutes.

The other night I sat back and watched one of my girls decorate one of my favorite desserts: chocolate cake—just plain old chocolate cake out of the box—I don't know if there's anything better on planet Earth. She made it and decorated it just right (and somehow mixed in a bunch of love.) Then she set it in the middle of the table ready to serve… that's about as close to heaven as you can get on earth. When all is well at the table, all else seems good too.

The table is a purpose place. The table within your home is a place that God has given you for intimacy and relational covenant, possibly greater than any other found in the home for your family.

Yes, the family is stronger when it's seated regularly around the table. Healthy marriages make for healthy homes, and healthy homes guarantee a healthy church community. Marriage is certainly a table where the love of Jesus is served. So is parenting. So goes the family, so goes the church, they are inseparable. Why? Because our kids are excitable: They are "capable of being awakened, aroused or stirred up to action." Their souls can be ignited when they experience love at the table.

INDISPENSABLE LOVE

It's amazing how much love permeates the New Testament. Once Jesus came on the scene, love took the spotlight in new ways. How do we let love permeates our home and our parenting?

Love Jesus.

It's that simple. No reason to overcomplicate things. If you love him with real love, everything else will follow. But its got to be real love. Not just some sentimental head nod. It's loving Jesus with all your heart, soul, mind and strength.

When you love somebody, you love what they love. For example, the Holy Spirit recently led me to buy a new bow. (I tend to sense this leading of God every fall, just before hunting season), I know it was the Lord, yet when I showed it to Cindy she was like, "You get suckered you into a new bow every year!" No, no, she didn't say that (But I could tell by the slight roll of her eyes that's what she was thinking.) She paused, took a little breath and said, "Let me see!" I showed her all the stuff on it that I loved and she acted like she genuinely cared. To her, I'm sure it looked just like the one the Spirit told me to buy last year, but she loved that bow too because she loved *me* and knew *I* loved it.

The point is simply this: if you love Jesus, you're going to love what he loves.

> Jesus replied, "Anyone who loves me will obey my teaching. My Father will love them, and we will come to them and make our home with them. Anyone who does not love me will not obey my teaching. These words you hear are not my own; they belong to the Father who sent me. —John 14:24-25

If we love him and love what he does, the kids will pick up on that. But it's not just for example or for show for your kids. Search your heart and make sure it's the real thing that you love because he first loved you, and that it's his love overflowing out of you.

And there are tons of ways that you can instill this love at the table. We'll get to that in just a little bit, but first of all let's take a reality pill.

BETRAYAL AT THE TABLE

Life is good when things are going well with the table. But life is not all chocolate cake. The table is often a place of bitterness. When you genuinely love your kids, you're going to be vulnerable. You can't love without exposing yourself to the possibility of getting hurt and things going really wrong. The people that will betray you the worst are the ones seated at the table close enough to kiss you. That's one of the risks of love: You open yourself up to be wounded. Scripture is full of examples of what can go wrong around the family table. Adam and Eve, Jacob and Esau, Joseph and there's more.

When you open up your heart at the table, your spouse, your kids and even strangers are going to be close enough to kick you in the shins or even stab you in the back while smiling at you. Big ouch. I'm telling you it's going to happen. It happened to Jesus and it's going to happen to us. Judas gets the award for how horribly wrong things can go at the table. Think about it. Jesus had spent three years with the disciples. By this point in his ministry, the disciples were like family... and yet Judas betrayed him *to the death* for a fistful of silver.

> In the same way, after the supper he took the cup, saying, "This cup is the new covenant in my blood, which is poured out for you. But the hand of him who is going to betray me is with mine on the table. The Son of Man will go as it has been decreed. But woe to that man who betrays him!" —Luke 22:20-22

*Some people feel that betrayal is the worst kind of wound, and I agree. You rarely see it coming. It's probably the closeness and the caring that makes its being so much. Other than our spouses, there's probably nobody closer and nobody we care about more than our kids. When things go wrong with them at the table—or worse yet, when they walk away from the table altogether, we take the wound.

What happens when your kids don't do what you think they should do? What happens when your kid doesn't turn out to be a doctor, a lawyer, or the president, or a missionary to Russia? What happens when you give your kids your all then it seems like you've lost them! You think to yourself, "What happened? What's going on here?" I don't know about you, but I want to hear from God's Word concerning that issue, because many of us have felt guilt, we've felt blame, we've felt the pain when your child goes on the run. ... Or maybe *you're* a child of God and you feel like *you're* on the run and think God won't forgive you? Either way, Jesus has a story for you in Luke chapter 15. It goes something like this:

> 7There was a man who had two sons, and he loved them like they were his own sons, because, well, they were. The younger one was the one who lived on the edge, and one day he decided to cross the line for good. "Father, give me my share of the estate." So the father divided his property between them. Soon,

the younger son got took the cash and he jetted. He set off for a distant country where he partied like crazy and blew it all.— Luke 15:1-13, (SOV, Shannon O'Dell Version.)

Chances are, in one way or another, you're going to have a "prodigal" someday.

What are some evidences that your son or daughter is on the run?

Number one: Self-centeredness. Babies and toddlers think only of themselves, but when an older kid acts like that all the time, and others in God don't matter, you got a prodigal at heart.

Number two: Know-it-all. Prodigals think they have all the answers. Don't bother offering advice or arguing with them. They honestly think you're as dumb as a brick.

Number three: Immediate gratification. When you see your child wanting what they want, when they want, there's a prodigal spirit in there. And in order to get what they want, they will squander the riches of God's grace, the riches of your family, and the riches of your love.

Prodigals display these symptoms in an incredible variety of ways across a broad range of intensity. Responding and treating these symptoms is as much an art as it is a science. I'm telling you, if there was some magic formula that could make them all right again, I'd be glad to write the book and make $1 billion. But simplistic answers simply don't exist. I know this firsthand because I'm in the thick of it. I love the beauty of watching my kids grow into what God has created them to be. Sometimes I smile, but sometimes it's tough. There's times when I just flat out cry or shout it out because it hurts when a prodigal is giving you fits. So what you do?

There is plenty wisdom to be gathered from those who've gone before us, and the word of God is filled with eternally significant examples and guidance. Let's start there, on our knees:

1. Pray for humility.

If you've got a prodigal son or daughter, the most important thing you can do at the beginning is to recognize that all of us were *and still are* prodigals. You might as well humble yourself right now, because that's probably one of the gracious reasons God is allowing your kid to go off the deep end. I was a nine-year-old prodigal and on the run. But from the end of road, I saw my Heavenly Father through the person of Jesus Christ, and he redeemed me and forgave me of my prodigal ways in March of 1981. But that spirit of self-centered, know-it-all, immediate gratification is alive and well in my flesh today. It's only by God's grace and by the power of his Spirit in me that I can walk the line. So when I see my kids crossing the line? I better be humble about it. So should you. Yes, we are parents, but we are first and foremost children—children of God.

> See what great love the Father has lavished on us, that we should be called children of God! And that is what we are!... Dear friends, now we are children of God, and what we will be has not yet been made known. But we know that when Christ appears, we shall be like him, for we shall see him as he is. —1 John 3:1-2

As God's kids, we are all excitable. God is still transforming us, showing we are "capable of being awakened, aroused or stirred up to action." Our souls too can be ignited when we experience love of God. That's why, in parenting, there is nothing more important than humbling yourself, finding a table and getting serious with God. When you understand his love, you'll understand better how to love your kids.

Follow God's example, therefore, as dearly loved children and walk in the way of love, just as Christ loved us and gave himself up for us as a fragrant offering and sacrifice to God.—Ephesians 5:1-2

God's love is tough sometimes. Right before Jesus invites us to dine with him, he says, "Those whom I love I rebuke and discipline. So be earnest and repent." Revelation 3:19. Most people haven't memorized *that* part of the passage!) Our love for our prodigal will include "rebuke and discipline" too, but it only works if it comes from that humble spirit of a parent that recognizes they too are a child.

2. Pray with transparency.

I think prayer should be transparent. That is, I think we should let our kids see our prayers and they should be able to see through our words to the love of God in us. We should be praying with our kids and over our kids. Paul gives us a great list to get started:

> *⁹ For this reason, since the day we heard about you, we have not stopped praying for you.*

- *We continually ask God to fill you with the knowledge of his will through all the wisdom and understanding that the Spirit gives,*
- *¹⁰ so that you may live a life worthy of the Lord and please him in every way:*
- *bearing fruit in every good work,*
- *growing in the knowledge of God,¹¹*
- *being strengthened with all power according to his glorious might*
- *so that you may have great endurance and patience,*
- *¹² and giving joyful thanks to the Father, who has qualified you to share in the inheritance of his holy people in the kingdom of light.* —*Colossians 1:9-12*

I think it's great to pray these things at the table, whether that's at breakfast or bedtime, you've got your kid captive at the table.

3. Pray that they'll get caught when they're guilty.

I know that sounds ugly, but for a prodigal, experience isn't just the best teacher, sometimes it's the *only* teacher that can get through. Check out what David wrote about himself in the Psalms 119:

> ⁶⁷Before I was afflicted I went astray, but now I obey your word...
> ⁷¹It was good for me to be afflicted so that I might learn your decrees.

⁷² The law from your mouth is more precious to me than thousands of pieces of silver and gold.

Rather than try to save our kids from the pain of their actions, it's almost always best to let them learn the hard way, particularly if they are know-it-alls. Ask God to rattle their cage and get their attention! That's the only thing that got through to the prodigal son:

> ¹⁴ After he had spent everything, there was a severe famine in that whole country, and he began to be in need. ¹⁵ So he went and hired himself out to a citizen of that country, who sent him to his fields to feed pigs. ¹⁶ He longed to fill his stomach with the pods that the pigs were eating, but no one gave him anything.--Luke 15:14-16

When my kids and my friends aren't walking with God I pray that consequences would come soon and severely. We're all too valuable to the Kingdom of God to be living aloof to the principles of God. The sooner we get spanked and get back on track, the better.

4. Pray for patience and keep "scoping."

Galatians 6:9 says, *"Let us not become weary in doing good."* So hang in there. In God's timing, you will reap a good harvest, but I can guarantee, it's going to happen on God's timetable and not yours. That's because he is going to be working on you as he works on them. It's amazing how a prodigal can be used by the Spirit to reveal pride, arrogance, and a judgmental spirit. You'll wish he would fix your kid today, but chances are he's not done with you yet.

The key to parental success when your kid is on the run, is the promise of their return. In Luke 15, the father saw his son "while he was still a long way off." He must have been on the watch, looking into the distance like a hunter searches a forest through his scope. When my kids have bombed, my natural tendency is to say, "Phhhhbb. What's the use? They're gonna do their own thing. Let'em go and let's get back to life." Wrong response. You have to continue the hope and continue the scope the horizon for their return.

5. Pray that they will come to their senses.

There's been times when—even as a child of God under the love of the Father and the compassion of His grace—that I've run like a prodigal. If you are humble, you'll admit that you have too. But here's the deal: If you are truly a child of God, you *will* come to your senses. If your kid is God's kid, they will too. It's a promise:

> "When he came to his senses, he said, 'How many of my father's hired servants have food to spare, and here I am starving to death! I will set out and go back to my father and say to him: Father, I have sinned against heaven and against you. I am no longer worthy to be called your son; make me like one of your hired servants.' So he got up and went to his father. —Luke 15:17-20

Christ's invitation to dine together never expires. He's always there waiting to fellowship and share life again at his table. Pray that he will allow your child to see the truth. Remember, our kids are excitable, they are "capable of being awakened, aroused or stirred up to action" just like we are. Never stop praying that God's Spirit will give them the wake-up call.

6. Love them unconditionally

> *"But while he was still a long way off, his father saw him and was filled with compassion for him; he ran to his son, threw his arms around him and kissed him. —Luke 15:20*

Is that not the most powerful picture? The father ran to him. And then it says, *"He threw his arms around him."* That kind of reception doesn't just happen. It happens because of forgiveness. Prodigals break our expectations and dreams. They drain us and wound us at our core. Please take that to the cross of forgiveness. You'll need to walk through forgiveness with them just like you do your spouse because those who sit closest to you are the ones who can hurt you the most. And remember: The pain of the wrong and the things you had to go through will be outweighed by the joy of their return.

> Therefore, as God's chosen people, holy and dearly loved, clothe yourselves with compassion, kindness, humility, gentleness and patience. Bear with each other and forgive one another if any of you has a grievance against someone. Forgive as the Lord forgave you. And over all these virtues put on love, which binds them all together in perfect unity.—Colossians 3:12-14

7. Celebrate at the table.

> "But the father said to his servants, 'Quick! Bring the best robe and put it on him. Put a ring on his finger and sandals on his feet. Bring the fattened calf and kill it. Let's have a feast and celebrate. For this son of mine was dead and is alive again; he was lost and is found.' So they began to celebrate.—Luke 15:22-24

When the kid leaves the table, it's appropriate, in some way, to celebrate at the table again when they return. Don't get me wrong. I'm not saying you just start over again like nothing happened. You need to forgive, absolutely. There will be a time for "rebuke and discipline" even if they are "earnest and repent." There may be serious consequences for their behavior, but let them know that you're on their team. Celebrate even small steps in the right direction. That's what our heavenly father does for us.

STARTING TODAY

Like I said, parenting is more art than science. But it's such a beautiful process. You've been given a piece of history to shape. You, as a child of God, are a piece of history too. God is shaping you and your family to build his Kingdom. We need to be sensitive to that and take it seriously! It's an incredibly important opportunity and responsibility and love is the first and most important leg.

A couple things you can do right now:

1. Order one of these awesome books that do a great job of describing the leg of love:
   - *How to Really Love Your Child* or *How to Really Love Your Teen* by Dr. Ross Campbell.
   - *The Five Love Languages for Children* or the *Five Love Languages for Teens* by Gary D. Chapman.
   - *Love Must Be Tough* by Dr. James Dobson.
   - *Who Switched Off My Brian* by Dr. Caroline Leaf

2. Start praying now. Don't put this off any longer. If your child is living in your home, regardless of the age, bring 'em together and pray every day. Now, I understand with busy schedules and carpools and football games and work and bla bla bla. It's time to put the excuses aside and go for it! This is one area where you can really be creative.
   - Send a prayer text.
   - Stick a prayer note in their binder.
   - Send a prayer bomb in an email.
   - Skype or facetime 'em.
   - And there's always those few moments at the end of the night when you tuck them in or lay a hand on their shoulder and pray God's blessings upon them.

You cannot pray what's on your heart, or use prompts from the truth of the Bible. I regularly pray Proverbs 1:10-12, for my kids.

> [10] My son, if sinful men entice you,
>   do not give in to them.
> [11] If they say, "Come along with us;
>   let's lie in wait for innocent blood,

let's ambush some harmless soul;
 [12] let's swallow them alive, like the grave,
  and whole, like those who go down to the pit;

Sometimes I pray Psalms 1:1-4 over them.

Blessed is the one
 who does not walk in step with the wicked
or stand in the way that sinners take
 or sit in the company of mockers,
 [2] but whose delight is in the law of the LORD,
  and who meditates on his law day and night.
 [3] That person is like a tree planted by streams of water,
  which yields its fruit in season…

3.   Schedule table-time. I just beg of you, take your calendar and prioritize three meals a week at the table with your family, minimum. Three meals a week. For some breakfast may be the best meal. For some it may be dinner. Or lunch out on the town. I know our schedules are demanding, but don't let someone else counter the moments that Jesus counted so important. If you do not calendar your time, it will be calendared for you.

Love is indispensable and prayer is so powerful. Establish that leg under your table of parenting and everything else that we're going to talk about the upcoming chapters will not only make sense, but it will excite your family at the table. You and your kids really are exciTABLE!

Holy Spirit of the living God,

Awaken me! Arouse me and stir me up to action. I ask that you would ignite the souls of my children! I can only love because you first love me. Make me hungry to feast on your love in a real and authentic way. Humble me as I parent my children, constantly reminding me that I am your child and that you are parenting me. Give me the grace to see difficult times with my kids as your gentle hand of reproof and discipline in my personal life. With open hands I release each of my children to you. I ask that when they go astray that they would quickly experience the consequences, that they would come to their senses, that I would be patient and love them unconditionally, and that one day we will all fees together again at your table of love

Amen.

AT THE TABLE WITH JESUS

Great parenting begins when we humble ourselves before God and wholeheartedly embrace the truth that we are first and foremost children of God, and that he is parenting us just like we want to parent our kids.

1. Get along with the Lord at a table. Find someplace quiet where you will be interrupted. Shut off the phone. Just rest for a few minutes.
2. Unload anything that's on your mind. Just give it to him to hold while the two of you talk about other things.
3. Feast on 1 John 3. Savor every phrase and digest every word. Pick out three or four of the most powerful truths that are speaking to you right where you are right now.
4. Vividly imagine these truths. For example, when John says "all who have this hope in him purify themselves, just as he is pure," you might imagine Christ standing before you in his resurrected glory, radiating his pure glory. Then look at yourself, and imagine that same fear look of glory all over you.
5. Pick out one thing that you believe God is calling you to do in light of all these truths. Submit them to him, confessing your complete dependence on the power of his spirit in your spirit to do what it is and he wants you to do.

FOR GROUP DISCUSSION

1. Skim back through this chapter. Pick out one thing that was a relatively new idea for you. Share it with the group. Why do you think that this idea was more important than the other things you read? Was this just an idea or did it have Scripture attached to it. Doesn't make a big difference to you?

2. Your group might be a Sunday school class, our small group Bible study, or maybe even just some friends at work who gather to talk. As part of your discussion of this chapter, ask each other to keep the rest of the conversation confidential. We went your group to become a place of "transparent prayer, where you can share safely the prodigal aspects of your life and your children. Then:
   - Pray for humility.
   - Pray with transparency.
   - Pray that they will get caught.
   - Pray that they will come to their senses.

AT THE TABLE WITH YOUR KIDS

Prepare a really special dinner as a celebration of your kids at the table—not because they've done anything, but just because. The goal is to commit a random act of unconditional love.

1. Don't tell them what's going on, but go all out! Use the finest dishes and crank out some awesome food. Light candles and ask everyone to dress up a little bit before they come.

2. Carefully tear out the next page of this book, and cut up the verses and those little prayers and put them in a bowl in a center the table.

3. Think about what really speaks love into the heart of your kid. Ask God for guidance he will show you what it is and how you are supposed to give it to them.
   - Do they like gifts?

- Do they like words that make them feel special?
- Do they like it when you do things for them?
- Do they like just hanging out and being together?
- Do they like hugs, scratches and backrubs?

Whatever it is that makes them feel loved, feed it to them there at the table. They will eat it up.

4. Tell them that you love him so much that you're going to begin to pray the truths of scripture over them, asking for the very best blessings of God.
5. Let them pick out one of the pieces of paper from the bowl. Then open your Bible to the passage and read it. Let them discuss but they think it means. Then pray that prayer over your kids while asking for God's biggest and best blessings in their lives.
6. Keep that bowl in the middle of the table and have them pick a verse everytime you are all together. It's a new tradition!

Table 2: Parenting

Leg #2: Honor

> "A son honors his father, and a servant his master. If I am a father, where is the honor due me? If I am a master, where is the respect due me?" says the LORD Almighty."

> —Malachi 1:6

accounTABLE [*uh*-koun-t*uh*-b*uh*l] *adjective*
1. responsible to someone or for some action; answerable
2. what we become when the awesomeness of honor and integrity flourishes at the table.

I feel a special confidence when I'm walking tight with God, don't you? You can feel it in your heart. You can sense it as circumstances line up with your desires momentum that builds when you're moving according to Biblical principles. Following the moment by moment of the Spirit.

I felt that confidence full force back when God was knitting my heart together with Cindy's. All the biblical criteria I had been looking for in a future mate she had in abundance. And it didn't hurt that she was totally hot (still is, by the way). Sparks were flying and the Spirit was moving. I felt like I was revved up at the stoplight of godly romance, ready to peel out. Cindy was seat belted in, ready for the ride. I had a full tank of testosterone supercharging my engine and an open road in front of the two of us. It was clearly time to get the show on the road.

Before we started rolling, however, I was looking forward to doing something that I had always dreamed of: I wanted honor my future father in law by asking for permission to pursue his daughter. When I told Cindy I wanted to talk to her dad first, it endeared her to me all the more. By showing honor to her father man-to-man, I was showing honor to her as well. I know that's not the way it normally happens in our culture anymore. I knew that honorable things are exceptional things, and I looked forward to making the gesture.

The journey was about to begin just as I had planned. Then, in an instant, it all stalled out. He said "no." And he didn't just say "no." He said, "No, no, no, no, no."

"I don't have a peace about this, Shannon. Do not pursue her. Don't call her. Don't even write letters to her. If your paths cross in ministry, so be it. But nothing more."

I was shocked at first. Stunned, really. It just didn't compute. I mean, come on, I had this all mapped out. I was trying to do something godly by asking him for his endorsement on my dreams. I had complete confidence that it was time to start moving in the same direction with Cindy. But then, BLAM! BLAM! BLAM! BLAM! No! No! No! No! This guy shoots out all four tires on my dreams bringing my life to screeching, smoking, skidding halt. Now I was stranded in the middle of the intersection, storming around, yelling, and kicking up dirt. I was like, *Dude, Nobody is ever going to call you about your daughter again! He's just gonna go out and do it. Forget you!* Many, many unprintable words and thoughts were flying around in my brain and plenty of them made it past my lips. For many nights I stared at the ceiling with my fist clenched in my jaw set.

It was decision time. I really was at a crossroads. One road led to Cindy. The other led to something I knew very little about: honor. In my vast 19 years of experience, I had assumed "honor" was a formality. It would take many months to learn that honor goes much, much deeper than that.

HONOR DEFINED

Dictionaries describe "honor" with words like *fairness, honesty, integrity in one's beliefs or actions.* Honor is also something that we do, by showing *high respect, worth and rank.* When it comes to the table of parenting, honor is something we want for our kids. Yeah, "respect, worth and rank" that's what we deserve, right?! That's what we should demand in our homes, right?! Hmmmm. Maybe it's time to think about that. Honor really does go much, much deeper than that.

If we want to see honor at the table in our home, we must first become accounTABLE, for honor always begins with personal, parental responsibility.

I'm telling you, if you embrace this concept of honor, it will radically shake the foundations of hell and change your world. Bringing honor to the table can be a catalyst, which starts a chain reaction of good in your family. When we become accountable to the timeless principles of God, when we begin to respect and follow the authorities that God has given us, *then* honor comes to the table.

- **HONOR ACKNOWLEDGES**
- **HONOR APPRECIATES**
- **HONOR ENCOURAGES**
- **HONOR COMPLIMENTS**
- **HONOR APPLAUDS**
- **HONOR SERVES**
- **HONOR ELEVATES EVERYTHING**

Everything goes better with honor. It's like mashed potatoes. I say serve it with everything: Marriage, business, school, neighborhood, church, sex, athletics, academics etc., etc., etc. Honor causes the quality of life to go up. When honor is at the table we go higher relationally, socially, morally, spiritually, and economically.

Honor may not be trendy, and it's certainly not vogue. It's more popular to be antiestablishment, but I'm voting for honor every time. But in our culture, we dishonor the honorable. We honor the dishonorable. We raise up junk, rebellion, and sell the stuff that shocks because that's what we buy.

Everyone wants honor, but very few get it. That sure is the way it is with parenting. Without the leg of honor under the table, nothing else seems to matter. But the more we want it, the less we seem to get it. What's wrong with this picture?

HONOR WHERE HONOR IS DUE

In the year 550 BC, the nation of Israel was in a downward spiral. The economy was down. Moral was down. The cities had become bastions of debauchery (that's a nasty sounding word, isn't it, "debauchery"). Things were bad and going in a worse direction fast. Sound familiar? It was the 21st century 21 centuries ago. Into this darkness, God spoke words of light through the prophet Malachi, illuminating the core of their problem:

> "A son honors his father, and a servant his master. If I am a father, where is the honor due me? If I am a master, where is the respect due me?" says the LORD Almighty."-- Malachi 1:6

The problem for the Israelites was the same problem that many of us face today: God had become commonplace.

Honor elevates things that are exceptional, but they weren't doing that with God. The holy majestic authoritative King of Kings and Lord of Lords and what his Word says has become ho-hum. That's lethal. Honor puts value on something. Honor makes something exceptional. We dishonor something by treating it as normal or common, and that's what so many of us do with God today. This is a huge problem for kids who have grown up in the church. They've been in church ever since they can remember. They've heard every sermon. They've sung every song. Their youth pastors have tried every trick in the book to snap them out of their trance. And perhaps worst of all, they don't see any fire in the lives of their parents. Yes, maybe "Jesus is in the house." Maybe everybody at one point invited him in to have dinner. If so, he's right there at the table. But does anybody even care?

> Jesus said to them, "Only in his hometown and in his own house is a prophet without honor." —Matt. 13:57

If your parenting has lost its edge, if your family has lost its fire, take your *own* pulse first. Where is *your* honor-meter pointing? Consider a major table moment that took place in the town of Bethany:

> Here a dinner was given in Jesus' honor. Martha served, while Lazarus was among those reclining at the table with him. Then Mary took about a pint of pure nard, an expensive perfume; she poured it on Jesus' feet and wiped his feet with her hair. And the house was filled with the fragrance of the perfume. But one of his disciples, Judas Iscariot, who was later to betray him, objected, "Why wasn't this perfume sold and the money given to the poor? It was worth a year's wages." He did not say this because he cared about the poor but because he was a thief; as keeper of the money bag, he used to help himself to what was put into it. —John 12:2-6

Any question about who gave honor that night? Maybe it's time to do something exceptional, something extravagant, something so out of the ordinary that everybody at the table of your house wakes up. Honor will radically blow your mind and put your faith on the line. This is the tale-tale sign of true obedience for Christ follower. It's the ticket to spiritual success. And it will radically impact everyone around you.

We need to be serious about being children of God so that we can raise up a generation of children that are passionate about God.

You can't have positive healthy relationships without honor. Ultimately, honor is found when you, as children of God, say "yes" and submit to the Father. Where do you start?

PRAYER

Prayer is honorable to God. I'm not just talking about reciting the Lord's Prayer at church or repeating a common blessing before every meal (though that can be a sincere part of it). Think of prayer this way: Jesus promised that he would always be with us and that he would be in us (Matthew 28:20, John 14:20). That means prayer can and should be an ongoing spiritual conversation with our awesome, ever-present Lord—a conversation that honors him moment by moment of every day by acknowledging his exceptional presence in us, and around us, without ceasing (1 Thessalonians 5:17).

GIVING

We also honor God with our resources... No, let me correct that, with *his* resources which he has entrusted to us to use for his honor.

> This will bring health to your bod and nourishment to your bones.

> Honor the LORD with your wealth, with the first-fruits of all your crops; then your barns will be filled to overflowing, and your vats will brim over with new wine. —Proverbs 3:8-10

The next time you're sitting at the table paying bills, make it worship! I help my kids understand how much their cell phones cost, by asking them to send me a verse from their daily Bible reading. No reading, no phone. I remind them their monthly cost and the verses start flowing again. Bring your kids into it and show them where God's resources are going. Together, ask God to bless your family's tithe. Brainstorm on worthy causes that you can invest in to bring glory to his name. He promises if we do this, we will have more than we need, so we can keep on giving more.

RESPECT

We honor God when we show respect for the leaders he has placed in our lives. Ultimately, we can't control whether our kids will respect us or not. But I'd say it's extremely unlikely that they will if we don't respect those God has commanded us to honor.

> "Obey your leaders and submit to their authority. They keep watch over you as men who must give an account. Obey them

so that their work will be a joy, not a burden, for that would be of no advantage to you."—Hebrews 13:17

That includes politicians and government officials. We don't have to agree with them, but we must show them honor.

"Everyone must submit himself to the governing authorities, for there is no authority except that which God has established. The authorities that exist have been established by God. Consequently, he who rebels against the authority is rebelling against what God has instituted, and those who do so will bring judgment on themselves."—Romans 13:1-2

Seriously, if our kids see us disrespecting leaders we disagree with, how can we expect them to respect us when they disagree with us? Just think about it.

HUMILITY

Honor isn't just about our actions. Honor is all about our heart. Check out another powerful table moment with Jesus:

> One Sabbath, when Jesus went to eat in the house of a prominent Pharisee, he was being carefully watched.[7]When he noticed how the guests picked the places of honor at the table, he told them this parable: [8]"When someone invites you to a wedding feast, do not take the place of honor, for a person more distinguished than you may have been invited. [9]If so, the host who invited both of you will come and say to you, 'Give this person your seat.' Then, humiliated, you will have to take the least important place.[10]But when you are invited, take the lowest place, so that when your host comes, he will say to you, 'Friend, move up to a better place.' Then you will be honored in the presence of all the other guests. [11]For all those who exalt themselves will be humbled, and those who humble themselves will be exalted."—Matthew 14:6-11

That's a straightforward verse from God's word. Want some more?!

> Wisdom's instruction is to fear the LORD, and humility comes before honor. —Proverbs 13:15

> Pride brings a person low, but the lowly in spirit gain honor.— Proverbs 29:23

> "Therefore the LORD, the God of Israel, declares: 'I promised that members of your family would minister before me forever.' But now the LORD declares: 'Far be it from me! Those who honor me I will honor, but those who despise me will be disdained. —1 Samuel 2:30

Listen, I could go on and on about this. Humility and honor are the Siamese twins of the Bible. This isn't odd; this is the way the Kingdom of God works. The humble are exalted. Those who first honor God are the ones that he honors. Are you getting this? We will get the verse about "children honor your father and mother" in just a little bit, but just remember:

- We have to be great kids so that we can raise great kids.
- Honor cannot be demanded. It must be earned.
- Honor is something your kids will give you when they catch it from you.
- Honor demanded is honor denied, but honor learned will be honor earned. You can demand honor when kids are little, but by the time they start growing hair all over, you better have earned it. If you try to demand honor that you haven't earned it's going to be a mess.
- If there's an honor problem at the table, we must check our own honor first. It's likely because we struggle in our honor of God. That's really the bottom line.

When honor is at the table, wow, I'm telling you it is sweet. A whole different atmosphere infuses the home.

¹⁵ Let the peace of Christ rule in your hearts, since as members of one body you were called to peace. And be thankful. ¹⁶ Let the message of Christ dwell among you richly as you teach and admonish one another with all wisdom through psalms, hymns, and songs from the Spirit, singing to God with gratitude in your hearts. ¹⁷ And whatever you do, whether in word or deed, do it all in the name of the Lord Jesus, giving thanks to God the Father through him. ¹⁸ Wives, submit yourselves to your husbands, as is fitting in the Lord. ¹⁹ Husbands, love your wives and do not be harsh with them. Children, obey your parents in everything, for this pleases the Lord. ²¹ Fathers, do not embitter your children, or they will become discouraged.—Colossians 3:15-21

That's about as simple a to-do list as you could ask for in godly parenting. It's also simply impossible to-do unless you are trusting in Christ to do it through you. These are the kinds of things that you cannot do in your own strength. But when we depend on him, all things are possible. Do your part first. By God's grace, you'll be opening the door and inviting your kids into an honorable life as well.

HOW TO BRING YOUR KIDS TO THE TABLE WITH HONOR

In Scripture we are sometimes commanded to obey "just because." God isn't obligated to give us any sort of rationale for what he does or tells us to do. (Just ask Job!). Cindy's dad owed me no explanation for his "no." Sometime, though, God does explain. He takes special care to give reasons to children for honoring their parents:

Children, honor your father and mother which is the first commandment with a promise. So that your life will go well and that you may live long on the earth.—Ephesians 6:2.

Every command of God has its benefits. The command to honor father and mother comes with a lot of them:

- **It Provides Protection.** When children place themselves under God-given leadership, the leadership creates an umbrella of safety for the child.
- **It Accelerates Maturity.** Children can't take a pill for maturity. They have to be serious about the Word of God and learning from those who have gone before them. Sure, everyone has to learn by experience, but life will go well and you'll live longer if you become teachable learning from others!
- **It Gives a Heightened Sense of Uniqueness.** There's a reason medals of Honor are given to so few people. They are special. The uniqueness of saying yes and honoring God's word makes you a standout.

Our kids are much more likely to experience these benefits if we take the initiative to make them a reality around the table. We don't want to *force* our kids to honor us at the table, but we can sure set the table in a way that *influences* them toward a life of honor.

1. Honor *your* Parents at the Table.

Honor starts in the heart and overflows into our actions. Or at least it should. I'll never forget a memorial service at our church for a very godly man. He had led a great family that I love with all my heart. He was a lover of Christ. I sometimes imagine that he's attending our services as one of the "great cloud of witnesses" in Hebrews 13. But that day, as his sons and daughters came by the casket, one of his children leaned over into the casket and said something I will never forget: "Dad I'm so sorry that I waited this long to invest in honoring you, I'm so sorry I waited this long."

They had spent thousands of dollars on a casket and on flowers and on a headstone and on pictures, *but they didn't do while he was alive.* They didn't honor him as they could have on earth.

Certainly, there's a powerful lesson in there for all: Why wait? Honor is something that we can bring to the table anytime, every time, all the time for any reason or no reason at all. Why wait?! Why not throw a special dinner for your parents for no other reason than to give them honor where they have earned it. Remember: honor acknowledges, appreciates, encourages, complements, applauds, serves and elevates everything that is good. Do it for your parents now, and who knows, maybe someday your kids will do it for you to.

2. Honor the Leaders of the table.

GenX parents have started catering to our children so much that they have come to expect the seat of honor at the table. That's biblical anarchy. Honor is earned, not demanded. I say it's time to demote the kids by training them to show simple expressions of honor to their leaders:

- Parents get the ends of the table.
- Parents get the first bite.
- Kid's get to do the dishes.

I'm not talking about putting kids down, just putting them in their place.

3. Honor the Provision on the table

Our church is doing a lot of work in Haiti right now. I pray that we are helping them. I know that they are helping us. You really don't look at a full plate of food the same when you seen a city full of people who have none. How do we increase our appreciation for the exceptional food God has supplied for us in this country?

- **Give thanks.** At the table during the Last Supper, Jesus took the bread, broke it, blessed it and gave thanks. Every molecule of food on our tables is a gracious provision from our great provider. Give him sincere thanks before taking a bite.

- **Control the menu.** Okay, this is a pet peeve of mine: Mom puts a gorgeous meal on the table, but little Joe there gets macaroni and cheese every time because that's all he likes. Well, little Joe needs to start learning how to eat broccoli, Amen? Don't tell me "macaroni and cheese is all he'll eat." Really? Give little Joe to me for four days. When kids learn to honor and eat what you place in front of them, they are also learning to honor and eat the truth that God places in front of them, even when they don't like it.

- **Serve Health.** Your meals are contributing to the future health of your children both physically and spiritually. What are you putting on the table? Is it processed? Is it microwaved? Is it quick stuff? Your physical food reflects the spiritual food you're providing for your kids at your spiritual table when they come to feast from your life. When you are feasting on the word of God and intimate times of prayer, then you have something to feed them. But if you're spiritual pantry is empty? The best he can do is offer fast food Christianity which makes them obese and lazy.

4. Honor your Kids around the Table.

Kids desire honor just like you do. You can respect them and bring honor to your table by developing a handful of habits:

- **Listen to them.** Make sure everyone around the table gets a chance to be heard without interruption.
- **Care about what they care about.** Learn about their friends. Talk about their favorite sports, books, bands, etc. etc.
- **Celebrate them.** One of my friends has a special "celebrate plate" that the kids get to eat off of when they've done something exceptional. It doesn't have to be a huge accomplishment, but a huge compliment inspires them and affirms them.
- **Enjoy them.** These years will not last forever. Lean back and cross your arms and enjoy your kids at the table.

- **Don't provoke them.** *⁴ Fathers, do not exasperate your children; instead, bring them up in the training and instruction of the Lord.--Ephesians 6:1.*
- **Pray for them.** I was having dinner at a friend's house and before the meal he made a special point to pray for his kids. I mean he *really* prayed biblical truth over his kids. "Lord Jesus, I want to thank you so much that my kids are the head and not the tail, the top not the bottom, blessing coming in, and blessed going out" (Deuteronomy 28). "Lord Jesus, I thank you that my kids are fearfully and wonderfully made" (Psalm 139), "God thank you that you have chosen them" (Colossians 3). Here's the deal. Proverbs 18:20 says, *"The power of life and the power of death are in the tongue"* When you speak you unleash the power to hurt or harm. Let your prayers coat your kids with life-giving truth.
- **Guard your thoughts about them.** Proverbs 4:23 says, ""Be careful how you think; your life is shaped by your thoughts." (GNT) Just because you think it doesn't make it true. So think thoughts God has promised for your children.

The end result of all of this is that God gets the praise and God gets the honor when the things that he honors are honored at the table. Everything we do around the table has the honor of God as the means and the end. Let there be nothing above him. Let everything be below him.

> "You are worthy, our Lord and God, to receive glory and honor and power, for you created all things, and by your will they were created and have their being."-—Revelation 4:11

We have a mission: To honor God. We have purpose: To honor God... And it's not prep time. It is go time.

THE REST OF STORY.

It took a good long while to get my wits about me after Cindy's dad denied me permission to pursue her. A lot of prayer, a lot of long walks, and couple of cold showers helped. Sixteen months had passed. Dare I say, a big boy became a young man during that time. I had survived the most intense disappointment and rejection of my life. In the aftermath, I had matured in a quantum leap as I wrestled with desire and denial. As the Spirit searched my heart and showed me my ways, I learned to place my confidence in God rather than myself. I learned that my security and identity come from Christ and not a girl or any other relationship, and I made the decision to serve the Lord in full-time ministry. God had captured my attention in new ways as I probed the depths of honor and what it meant to honor those he honors

After I turned 21, my path crossed with Cindy's again. We were at a retreat center for a couple weeks of training at the home base of a revival ministry. All the feelings and desires I had buried came back. But this time, it was different. It was different because *I* was different. Now, a year and a half later, I felt the confidence of walking with the Lord again, but even that was different. This time it was mixed with humility. Over the last year and a half, honor had taken me deeper than I had ever gone before.

After several days of focus prayer, I knew it was time to honor Cindy's father one more time. This time, it was no formality. No cockiness, no assumptions; this was real. I was pursuing a relationship with Cindy's father so that I could pursue an earthly bride. But the Spirit was really asking me to pursue my heavenly Father to develop *his* ministry and develop His bride.

Not at all certain of what the answer would be, I picked up the phone and dialed. This time, he said, "Yes. Shannon, I sense and discern what God has done in your life. I'm very much ready to give you permission to pursue my daughter."

The next thing I knew, I was sitting across the table from Cindy at Olive Garden babbling like a giddy kid. Ten months later, I was at another table in a restaurant south of Memphis, weeping as Cindy's father and mother gave me their blessing to marry their daughter.

That's just about everything that I know about honor, and what it means for children to honor parents and, ultimately, honor God. Oh, and I do know one other thing: If some punk 19 year old kid comes asking about my daughter, he better be ready.

Holy Father, You are worthy, my Lord and God, to receive glory and honor and power. You created all things. By your will they were created and have their being. I sincerely ask, in the name of Jesus and by the power of your Holy Spirit in me, that you would be honored at my table, that my kids experience that honor and choose to honor you in all that they do.

Amen.

AT THE TABLE WITH JESUS

- Read and ponder Colossians 3:1-21. What parts of this passage seem to be speaking to you the loudest?
- Pour out your heart to the Lord and declare your dependence on Christ and the presence of the Holy Spirit in you to make this happen.
- Review the section about the ways we, as individuals can honor God. Then:
- Pray. Communicate openly and continually with Christ, honoring his presence as radically exceptional.
- Give. Ask the Spirit to show you the specific ways he wants you to give God's resources in order to bring him honor. Be open to him leading you in unique ways.
- Respect. Consider all the leaders God has placed over you. How can you tangibly show God honor by honoring them?
- Humility. Read Matthew 14. What does God seem to be showing you about yourself in this parable?

FOR GROUP DISCUSSION

Skim over this chapter and pick out something that you've never really thought about before. Share it with your group.

Evaluate these two phrases:

- We have to be great kids so that we can raise great kids.
- Honor cannot be demanded. It must be earned.

Restate each phrase using your own words.

Do you think these are true in 1) every situation, 2)some situations, 3) no situations.

Give examples to support your answer.

Read Malachi 1.

What similarities to you see with the Israelites in this passage and your country, city, church and family?

What could you, as a group, do to honor God by honoring your parents, leaders, provision and kids?

AT THE TABLE WITH YOUR KIDS

Read John 12:1-19 as a family, with each person reading one verse at a time.

Identify all the main characters in the passage.

Assign someone to be the narrator, then someone to do each of the different voices.

Re-read it as dramatically as possible.

Which characters wanted to make Jesus "common?" Which characters wanted to honor Jesus by doing something exceptional? Which character are you most like?

Brain storm on crazy things you could do to bring Jesus honor.

Table 2: Parenting

Leg #3: Training.

> "He is wooing you from the jaws of distress to a spacious place free from restriction, to the comfort of your table laden with choice food."

> —Job 36:16

irrefuTABLE [ih-ref-yuh-tuh-buh l, ir-i-fyoo-tuh-buh l]
1. Incapable of being refuted or disproved; indisputable
2. Unchangeable

When comes to priorities in training our kids, I think most of us are only about 180° off. We're close—except that everything on the top of the list should be on the bottom, and everything on the bottom should probably be on the top. Other than that I think we're doing pretty well.

Sarcasm aside, take an honest look at what we prioritize: education, sports, and entertainment. There's nothing wrong with any of those things. In fact, God endorses them all at different places in the Scriptures. And let's face it; we love it when our kids excel in these areas because it really makes us look good in public. But God is far more concerned about what's happening in the privacy of our own heart. Do our priorities match his?

[19] "Do not store up for yourselves treasures on earth, where moths and vermin destroy, and where thieves break in and steal. [20] But store up for yourselves treasures in heaven, where moths and vermin do not destroy, and where thieves do not break in and steal. [21] For where your treasure is, there your heart will be also... [24] "No one can serve two masters. Either you will hate the one and love the other, or you will be devoted to the one and despise the other. You cannot serve both God and money... [31] So do not worry, saying, 'What shall we eat?' or 'What shall we drink?' or

'What shall we wear?' ³² For the pagans run after all these things, and your heavenly Father knows that you need them. ³³ But seek first his kingdom and his righteousness, and all these things will be given to you as well. —Matthew 6:19-24, 31-33

Honestly, aren't the vast majority of the stressors in our life because we have our priorities screwed up? We're *so* focused on the things that are not that important. We spend our money and time and passions running here and there trying to get this and that and provide our kids with everything that they need to be "successful". We're going so fast that we rarely rest, rarely refocus on the things that have never ending value and honor. When Job's life was so messed up, Elihu, one of his buddies, had the wisdom to help him put things in perspective:

> ² "Bear with me a little longer and I will show you that there is more to be said in God's behalf. ³ I get my knowledge from afar; I will ascribe justice to my Maker. ⁴ Be assured that my words are not false; one who has perfect knowledge is with you…¹⁶ "He is wooing you from the jaws of distress to a spacious place free from restriction, to the comfort of your table laden with choice food."—Job 36:2-4, 16

In the midst of all his illness, death, bankruptcy, and pain, Elihu told Job that God was gently releasing him from all the things that had consumed his attention. Aod was inviting Job to the table, just like Jesus did for us.

Put yourself in Job's shoes for a moment. (Well, actually at this point he didn't even have any shoes. Just a bunch of festering boils on his skin, but you know what I mean.) Imagine all of the things that are bringing distress to you right now. Can you list them? Now, feel the gentle touch of a friend on your cheek as he tells you God is wooing you away from that and inviting you to the table. Because that's what God is doing right now. He is gently calling all of us to get our priorities straight and to focus our lives first on the things that matter the most and that bring us true life. A different version words it like this:

> "Oh, Job, don't you see how God's wooing you from the jaws of danger? How he's drawing you into wide-open places—inviting you to feast at a table laden with blessings? —Job 36:16 (MSG)

If you get that picture in your mind, it will truly be unforgettable. Not only that, but we have the incredible opportunity to parent in a way that trains our kids to forget about the things that don't matter and to seek first that, which is unforgettable: God's kingdom.

It's all about priorities. Christ is first, irrefutably. For me personally, this is a constant hurdle. Keeping my priorities straight is a minute-by-minute, day-by-day process of reminding of myself, through the leadership of the Holy Spirit that I am influencing my children to be world changers. We are making disciples. You should see it that way too. God has given you a piece of history. Kids are "history in the making." Our kids will shape history for good or bad and God has entrusted their training to us. This is why the table of parenting is so vital, and why this third leg, the leg of training, is so indispensable:

God, in his sovereign grace, has entrusted us with kids, divine pieces of history, that we are to train to make a difference that will count for eternity.

> Fathers, do not exasperate your children; instead, bring them up in the training and instruction of the Lord. —Ephesians 6:4

BUT, BUT, BUT...

I know what you're feeling right now. I really do, because that's what I feel too. Whenever I see this challenge in Scripture, my immediate response is one of intimidation. *How in the world can I do that when I don't do it myself and when I fall short so often? I'm just going to punt to the Sunday school teacher, or student pastor. I'm just going to pray for the best...*

Listen, if you're feeling inadequate to train your kids, you are absolutely right. You can't do it. In fact, you weren't designed to do it. You're incompetent! And that's the way, God planned it:

⁴ Such confidence we have through Christ before God. ⁵ Not that we are competent in ourselves to claim anything for ourselves, but our competence comes from God. ⁶ He has made us competent as ministers of a new covenant—2 Corinthians 3:4-6

Training your kids starts with this confession: *Lord I can't do this, but you can. And you live in me. My life is your life. I'm trusting you to do it through me.*

That's where training begins and that's where training ends too: Trusting in the Lord rather than your own strength and abilities. God designed the Christian life to be lived this way to guarantee that the glory for anything good that happens goes to God. The idea that God only chooses and uses people who have their act together is a lie from Satan. Check out this table-moment Jesus had and you'll see:

²⁷ Jesus went out and saw a tax collector by the name of Levi sitting at his tax booth. "Follow me," Jesus said to him, ²⁸ and Levi got up, left everything and followed him.²⁹ Then Levi held a great banquet for Jesus at his house, and a large crowd of tax collectors and others were eating with them. ³⁰ But the Pharisees and the teachers of the law who belonged to their sect complained to his disciples, "Why do you eat and drink with tax collectors and sinners?"³¹ Jesus answered them, "It is not the healthy who need a doctor, but the sick. ³² I have not come to call the righteous, but sinners to repentance."—Luke 5:27-32

Seriously, if you look at the people that Jesus hung out with at the table, there was really only one requirement: you had to be really messed up. Jesus hung out with messes. Our kids need to know that. We need to remember that. He didn't come to dine with healthy people, he came to dine with the sick ones who knew they couldn't do it on their own.

Don't think for a second that I always have my act together at my house. My house regularly has the smoldering's of an earthquake. We are always battling huge issues—crazy issues that you wouldn't think a pastor is supposed to deal with. I know for me personally, there's so many things that I've need to change in my approach to parenting. When I think about "training" I have to look back and ask, "What does this look like in my own life? Am I submitting as a kid so that my kids submit?" I encourage you, as Christ followers, to be transparent about these things. It's time to take off our masks and quit pretending that we have it all together. *Nobody* does. You can try to fake it in your own strength, but the Christian life really boils down to this: the grace of God and the power of his Spirit living through us.

If you're a child of God, you must realize that you're a piece of history as God's child as well. He's not done with you. You're not here just to be saved and then be done. You're here to shape God's plan. God is sovereign; it's up to him, but He wants to use you. His Spirit is in you and he has chosen to use you to make the difference. He wants to shape you to shape your kids in a way that allows their lives to change eternity through His power. There is no limit on what God can do through you as his child. The only limit is the one you put on God. So don't limit Him. *Trust* him.

Let's start with just a couple of irrefutable training Principles:

1. **Lead Intentionally.** Training will not happen unless you are intent on making it happen. It's highly unlikely that your children will figure this out on their own. I have seen rare exceptions where God raises a child up out of a very dark, difficult, sinful situation. Most of the time kids are trained because the parent is intentionally setting priorities, training and leading in the home.

2. **Lead with Initiative.** What do you want to do? What do you want be? What do you want to see happen? God is ready to use you to do these things, you just must humbly submit and then step out in strategic faith to see it happen.

3. **Lead Indirectly.** Kids are more likely to be trained by what you do rather than what you say. It's called modeling. Ephesians 5:1 says, *"Be an imitator of Christ."* 1 Corinthians 11:1 says, *"Follow my example as I follow the example of Christ Jesus."* For example,

we want to train our kids to be part of a vibrant community of believers on a regular basis. Statistics tell us that if both Mom and Dad take their kids to church, 72% of those kids will attend church as adults. If Dad takes the kids to church, 55% of kids will go to church as adults. But if Mom is the only one going to church with their child, only 15% of those kids will attend as adults. (Think about that, dads!) If Mom and Dad are CEO attenders (CEO stands for Christmas and Easter, Only), 86% of their kids will never attend church after turning 18.

4. **Lead Immediately.** Yesterday is history and tomorrow never comes. Today is all you've got. You might think it's too late. Maybe your kid is already a legal adult. All I can say is that don't let arbitrary American numbers influence you're training. There's nothing magical about turning 18 in God's kingdom. What are we supposed to say? "Happy birthday to you! God bless you! I'm done with you!" I think 18 is a great age to get them on their feet, be responsible, have vocational focus and vision and all those things. But you still have influence. After they "leave and cleave" you're wise if you don't get in their business, but you can still lead indirectly by modeling. It's going to be more "show" than "tell" at this point. (Unless they ask you for advice, I'd give it very, very sparingly.) Your children will always be observing you, as a child of God, and learning from your example.

The keys to training are leading intentionally, with initiative, while modeling indirectly by starting immediately. And the awesome thing about it is we have the best book the universe to tell us the next steps.

THE TRAINING MANUAL IN THE TRAINING MANUAL

God's word is the beginning and the end of all godly training. That book has proven itself over and over again to be living, active and authoritative in all aspects of life. Not only that, but tucked right in the middle of the Bible is a specific book that was written specifically to train kids. Solomon was the son of David. He was arguably the wealthiest and wisest man that has ever lived. In the prime of his life he wrote the book of Proverbs—31 chapters of pointed, powerful, practical wisdom. He wrote it to his kids, and now it is been passed down so that we can share it with our kids.

Proverbs 22:6 says, *"Train a child in the way he or she should go, and in the end, when they are old, will not depart from it."* The word "train" in the original Hebrew means "to dedicate" and "to initiate." That's so powerful, because that's exactly what God does with each of us as his children. His spirit in us draws us into a dedicated relationship with God where he continually initiates us into his ways as he draws us to himself and into daily repentance.

The Proverbs are loaded with training material about the most practical and important aspects of life. Here are seven samples that I feel are very important:

Number 1: Train them to carefully select their friends. You want to make sure your kid's best friends are quality individuals that are shaping their future. I'm not saying they don't reach out to the lost and those that are hurting.

> Walk with the wise and become wise, for a companion of fools suffers harm. Trouble pursues the sinner, but the righteous are rewarded with good things. —Proverbs 13:20-21.

Number 2: Train your kids how to manage God's money.

The book of Proverbs is jam-packed with tons of excellent training

about how we should view money, get money, save money and give money.

Honor the LORD with your wealth, with the first fruits of all your crops; then your barns will be filled to overflowing, and your vats will brim over with new wine.—Proverbs 3:9-10

Do not wear yourself out to get rich; do not trust your own cleverness. Cast but a glance at riches, and they are gone, for they will surely sprout wings and fly off to the sky like an eagle.—Proverbs 23:4-5

Everywhere I look in Scripture, the power of the table as a place of training is evident. It really is amazing how training happens when people simply meet with Jesus at the table. Check out this table moment Jesus had with a man, and how it transformed the man's approach to money:

Jesus entered Jericho and was passing through. ²A man was there by the name of Zacchaeus; he was a chief tax collector and was wealthy... ⁵When Jesus reached the spot, he looked up and said to him,"Zacchaeus, come down immediately. I must stay at your house today."⁶So he came down at once and welcomed him gladly.⁷All the people saw this and began to mutter, "He has gone to be the guest of a sinner." ⁸But Zacchaeus stood up and said to the Lord, "Look, Lord! Here and now I give half of my possessions to the poor, and if I have cheated anybody out of anything, I will pay back four times the amount." ⁹Jesus said to him, "Today salvation has come to this house, because this man, too, is a son of Abraham. ¹⁰For the Son of Man came to seek and to save the lost."—Luke 19:2, 5-10

After his encounter with Zacchaeus, Jesus did more training about the use of money in God's kingdom. That's helpful, yet Zacchaeus' story reveals one of the most powerful training principle of all: When messed up people spend time at the table with Jesus, he changes them for the better.

Number 3: Train them to watch their words. Don't let your kids just say anything they want. Words are powerful. Show them the power of their words by modeling encouragement and speaking the truth. And I say it's time to dump the double standard. The Bible says that some words are "unwholesome." If your kids shouldn't say certain words, you shouldn't say them either.

Keep your mouth free of perversity; keep corrupt talk far from your lips. —Proverbs 4:24

Whoever conceals hatred with lying lips and spreads slander is a fool. Sin is not ended by multiplying words, but the prudent hold their tongues. The tongue of the righteous is choice silver but the heart of the wicked is of little value. —Proverbs 10:19-20

Number 4: Train them to be responsible.

Go to the ant, you sluggard; consider its ways and be wise! It has no commander, no overseer or ruler, yet it stores its provisions in summer and gathers its food at harvest. Proverbs 6:6-8.

I'm afraid we have lost the generation of hard workers. Yes, there's a few GenXers who are working hard, but many have lotion hands. We just think if we go to college we've got it made. Not anymore. You can go to college all you want and you can get all the degrees you want and have no heat. You must have attitude and you must have work ethic. I don't care where you graduated. I want to know if you can work. We have taught people that school work rather than hard work gets you paid excellently. That's wrong and it's un-Biblical.

The Bible says "children are a blessing." You know what they are blessed to do? Wash the dishes, mow the lawn, and buy your meal once in a while.

Number 5: Train them to guard their hearts.

Above all else, guard your heart, for everything you do flows from it. —Proverbs 4:23

A child's heart and mind are extremely valuable and extremely vulnerable. Train them to protect them. Don't just allow anything to come in their minds. Filter what they read and what they watch on television. Make sure any device with Internet access can only be viewed through passwords in a non-private part of the house. Broken bones and bruises will heal themselves. When a kid's heart and mind take a hit, the damage will probably stay with them forever in one way or another. So teach them to protect their own hearts and minds too.

Number 6: Train them to be generous.

One person gives freely, yet gains even more; another withholds unduly, but comes to poverty. A generous person will prosper; whoever refreshes others will be refreshed.—Proverbs 11:25.

Most kids' first word is "Mama." The first word of one of my kids was "mine!" Sound familiar? It does to me, because it sounds like me. Most of us were never really trained that *nothing* is "mine," and that *everything* is God's. But it is. Everything that we have is just on temporary loan to be used for his honor and glory. Like almost everything else we've talked about in this book, generosity can be taught, but it's better to be caught. If you want your kids to get it, just get into it yourself and bring them along for the ride. Generous giving is a blast. Discovering where God wants you to give next is part of the adventure. It builds faith in God's provision. It builds ownership in the kingdom. And you know what? It's not all about you. It really does matter to the people on the receiving end.

Number 7: Train them to fear God.

Hopefully you know that I'm not talking about using God as some sort of black cloud of impending punishment, ready to strike with his lightning bolts every time your kid steps on the line. No, I'm not talking about scaring them with God. We're talking about living in vibrant awareness of all the attributes of God—truths that should leave us in "awe"—because that's what the word "fear" means.

In the biblical context of Almighty God, that's what parental training and the book of Proverbs is all about. From cradle to graduation, we have only 216 months to have these table moments as the prioritized care giver, so let's do this right and make it irrefutable.

[2] for gaining wisdom and instruction; for understanding words of insight; [3] for receiving instruction in prudent behavior, doing what is right and just and fair; [4] for giving prudence to those who are simple, knowledge and discretion to the young— [5] let the wise listen and add to their learning, and let the discerning get guidance— [6] for understanding proverbs and parables, the sayings and riddles of the wise. [7] The fear of the LORD is the beginning of knowledge, but fools despise wisdom and instruction.—Proverbs 1:2-7

Number 8: Train them to Go.

Train up a child in the way he should go… —Proverbs 22:6

Give your kid a vision to leave, and live out their passion and purpose for life. Living in your basement at 25 years old is not cool. Getting to gold level on Xbox is not something to be desired, When it's time to go shopping, make sure they have worked as hard for their shoes as you have yours. If you have kids living at home when they are 30-something, move and ask him to take over the mortgage.

Oh Lord,

Train me to train my kids now. I'm trusting in you to do this through me, for I am inadequate without you. With you, however, I truly believe that all things are possible. Give me the willingness to step out in faith. Make my life a model to my kids so that when they see me they see you working through me. Guide us in your word for ultimate truth and instruction.

Amen.

AT THE TABLE WITH JESUS

Start out by spending a little time thanking God for the truth in these passages:

- 1 John 1:8-10—all of us are "messed up" by sin. When we admit that to God he forgives us and cleanses us.
- Romans 8:1—No one who is in Christ Jesus is condemned by God.
- John 15:5—We can't do anything good without Christ doing it through us.
- Philippians 4:13—All things can be done through the strength of Christ.

Read Matthew 6:24-34. Let the Holy Spirit of God really test your heart.

- What are your main worries?
- How would your life be different if you completely trusted God with these concerns?
- If believed that God would take care of tomorrow, how would it change your actions today?
- Prayerfully contemplate what it would mean to you if you were to "seek first the kingdom of God and his righteousness."
- Talk to Jesus about these things. Be transparent and totally honest with him. He knows you and he loves you and wants to train you in new ways.

FOR GROUP DISCUSSION

Have everyone skim over this chapter.

- Pick out the most important thing they learned.
- Was there something that stood out to most people in the group? Or did everybody up with something unique?
- Are these principles for individuals or could they also be applied by your whole group?

Read the accounts of these two table moments others had with Jesus getting the full context:

Luke 5:27-39

Luke 19:1-27

- Do you see any repeated themes?
- What principles can you pull from these passages that would be great for training kids?
- How could those lessons be presented creatively to make them irrefuTABLE?

AT THE TABLE WITH YOUR KIDS

The table forces communication. I like that. Face-to-face with each other, with mouths full of food most of the time, and the no-talking-with-your-mouth-full rule in place, the table is also a great place to listen. In addition to that, I would like to encourage and enforce a no-cell-phone rule at the table. Incessant texting, nonstop twitter, news checking and flinching every time Facebook updates should be banned. Children shouldn't be allowed to have their cell phones at the table either. Table time is sacred time. Protect it from here on out, okay?

Proverbs comes in 31 chapters. That's one for every day of the month with an extra or two thrown in every once in a while. Coincidence? Maybe, but it is a convenient excuse to transform your dining room table into a full-blown spiritual training table every day of the month.

1. Get one Bible for every person that's going to be at the table, just by a couple of the inexpensive ones that you can keep around for a while.
2. After a meal, read the Proverb that corresponds to the day of the month. Have everyone read it silently to themselves.
3. Each person at the table then gets a chance to pick out the specific passage that they feel is most important for the family at that given moment.
4. Probe the passage with good open-ended questions:

- Why did they pick out one passage out of all the possible passages?
- What do you think motivated Solomon to write it?
- Is the passage as relevant today as it would have been 3000 years ago when it was written?
- What are possible ways to specifically apply to train principle in this passage?
- What could be done as a family and as individuals to make it a reality?

Table 2: Parenting

Leg #4: Truth

> He humbled you, causing you to hunger and then feeding you
> with manna, which neither you nor your ancestors had known,
> to teach you that man does not live on bread alone but on every
> word that comes from the mouth of the LORD...

> —Deuteronomy 8:3

delecTABLE [de-lec-t*uh*-b*uh*l]
1. Highly pleasing, fit or suitable for eating.
2. biblical truth that can be mentally absorbed, consumed emotionally,
   ingested, and spiritually applied at the table.

A healthy family is a lot like a healthy corporation. As the dad
of a family, I see myself as the CEO, the Chief Executive Officer.
I'm responsible for everything that happens; I'm where the buck stops
and I need to be the one who takes the primary lead when it comes to
vision. Cindy is definitely the COO, the Chief Operations Officer.
Without her, the whole thing would blow apart and go up in flames in
a matter of minutes. We work together to fulfill the role of CFO, Chief
Financial Officer. But I always remember that our kids have a stake in
this corporation too.

As CEO, it's my job to protect, defend and direct our little
corporation, and I take a lot of pride in that job, actually. When I
recently realized what I had allowed to happen in my home, I have
to admit that I was embarrassed at first. Then I felt a real sense of
loss. And then I got pretty mad for letting it happen under my watch.
Finally, I decided to do something about it: I called a board meeting of
everybody who has stock in our tribe-- I guess you could have called it
a "family shareholders meeting."

First, I sent out an official announcement (whistled down the hall),
gathered everyone around the conference table (actually the coffee table

in the living room) and called the meeting to order. Then I shared a lot of the awesome stuff that I saw happening. (It's a good idea to affirm the positive before you have to confront the negative.) And then, I took full responsibility for the problem: I had allowed Satan to deceptively detour our family from our prime purpose. We were settling for what was temporarily good but had lost sight of want was eternally essential. The problem is so obvious to me now, but I was blind to it. It's crazy, really, that I didn't see it. Here's the deal:

As parents, we'll sign our kids up without asking them for ball, sign 'em up for cheer, sign 'em up for dance, and sign 'em up for this and that. We make them go to school. We make them practice their instrument. We tell them that they need to be committed to their team. We say, "Get your homework done!" And we make them open their history, their algebra, trigonometry, their biology, their English…

Now, there's nothing wrong with any of those things. My kids are involved in all those things and I make them study like they should. That's all well and good. But what I had done, as CEO, was allow the "earthly good" to take priority over the "eternally essential." We had erected an impressive table of parenting on love, honor and training, but we had neglected the leg of Truth. Decision by decision, we had encouraged—and even trained—our kids to put their textbooks on *top* of their Bibles and their academics *before* their faith. We made sure that they learn their facts and formula, but because our family is just as busy as yours, our kids were not getting through their pile textbooks to the Bible at all. Make all ball practices, and maybe a handful of student services.

I had let the Word of God, the living truth of Scripture, get buried under a bunch of academic stuff. There's really no excuse for that, but if it's any consolation, the Scriptures themselves showed me that I wasn't alone.

THE BUSY AND THE BEST

2500 years ago the walls of the holy city of Jerusalem were in shambles. God called Nehemiah in his people to right this wrong. It's an incredible account of determination, faithfulness, and sacrifice. Yet in the process, they seem to have let their busyness get the best of them. In the midst of all their work, the word of God had gotten buried. So Nehemiah called his own shareholders meeting.

> [1] all the people came together as one in the square before the Water Gate. They told Ezra the teacher of the Law to bring out the Book of the Law of Moses, which the LORD had commanded for Israel...[3] He read it aloud from daybreak till noon as he faced the square before the Water Gate in the presence of the men, women and others who could understand. And all the people listened attentively to the Book of the Law.[4] Ezra the teacher of the Law stood on a high wooden platform built for the occasion...[6] Ezra praised the LORD, the great God; and all the people lifted their hands and responded, "Amen! Amen!" Then they bowed down and worshiped the LORD with their faces to the ground... [8] They read from the Book of the Law of God, making it clear and giving the meaning so that the people understood what was being read...[9] For all the people had been weeping as they listened to the words of the Law. [10] Nehemiah said, "Go and enjoy choice food and sweet drinks, and send some to those who have nothing prepared. This day is holy to our Lord. Do not grieve, for the joy of the LORD is your strength."[11] The Levites calmed all the people, saying, "Be still, for this is a holy day. Do not grieve." [12] Then all the people went away to eat and drink, to send portions of food and to celebrate with great joy, because they now understood the words that had been made known to them.—Nehemiah 8:1-12

I was grieved too when I realize that I had neglected the word of God. Yet just like Nehemiah's tribe, a massive celebration awaits any family. We use the Word, at the table, to serve Jesus, the living water and the bread of life. In that sense, the living Truth of Scripture is fully eatable-- it's right and good to serve it to our kids as the most essential food group for life. By the guidance of the Spirit in them, our kids are capable of ingesting is eternal transforming truths. But they can't feast on his Word unless it's at the table. That's the best thing that we can make our kids to do, no matter how busy we are. A personal time in God's presence daily.

HOW DID WE GET HERE?

There's really no excuse for letting the word of God get buried in our lives. But there are certain mentalities that have made it easier for us to justify letting it happen.

1. **Drive-Through mentality.**
    Good churches serve the Word of God to their people with excellence. Sometimes, that becomes an excuse for us not feeding ourselves or our families. Just drive in and out once a week and call it good, right?

2. **TV tray mentality.**
    Some parents set their kids in front of Christian entertainment hoping it will provide spiritual nourishment. It's the Christian version of a TV dinner. The strategy is to push the kid into youth group, or camps, or concerts with high entertainment value, hoping that somewhere along the way they might take a bite of truth as well. You don't stop encouraging those things, but they are the accent to what is already being feed at the table in your home.

3. **The Pot-Luck mentality**
    Potlucks are awesome… once in a while. I love gathering at the table with friends to sample the stuff they're eating. But if that's the only way you eat, you'll never learn to cook up a balanced meal on your own. Same goes with our intake of scriptural truth. If we only eat what other people bring to the table, we might not ever discover how to feed ourselves what we truly

need-- all we can eat is what other people bring, rather than taking the lead to "bring it" ourselves.

4. **The Pre-chewed mentality**

    Back in the day, a late-night weekend comedy show did a skit called "Pre-Chewed Charlie's"—an advertisement for a restaurant for people that didn't like to chew their own steak. You guessed it: the waiters chewed it for them. Funny and disgusting. Unfortunately, that's how many of us get our regular intake of the Word of God. Some depend far too much on preachers and teachers to chew up and digest the word of God for them rather than feasting on the pure words themselves.

5. **The bar-bouncing mentality.**

    I remember back when bars and bar stools became the cool thing in houses. They were convenient for sure, but when you sat at the bar, you didn't have to talk to anybody face to face or look them in the eye. Some of us do the same thing with God in our study of the Scriptures. We don't want to look across into his eyes. We don't want to be honest about what we do and how we serve and being committed to the faithful call of God to build his church, to give, to tithe, to serve, to obey. We remove the emotions from it. We don't want to really get that involved or committed to God so we just give him this bar mentality and sit beside him instead of across from him. Interestingly, I don't see any bars in the Bible and there's no bar in Heaven. It's a table—and the table is designed for connection, intimacy, and feasting.

JOINING THE FEAST

The Bible offers a full-blown smorgasbord of truth and wisdom for life. It's like a huge buffet, lined with the very best of the very best of spiritual nourishment. There's meat and potatoes with salads galore topped off with refreshing drinks and sweet desserts. It's all eatable.

It's all beneficial. It's all profitable for teaching and for training and for correction and for reproof. Whether you are a spiritual infant, or think that you are mature and wise, the Bible has just what you need at every age.

> Therefore, rid yourselves of all malice and all deceit, hypocrisy, envy, and slander of every kind. Like newborn babies, crave pure spiritual milk, so that by it you may grow up in your salvation, now that you have tasted that the Lord is good. —1 Peter 2:1-3

> [11] We have much to say about this, but it is hard to make it clear to you because you no longer try to understand. [12] In fact, though by this time you ought to be teachers, you need someone to teach you the elementary truths of God's word all over again. You need milk, not solid food! [13] Anyone who lives on milk, being still an infant, is not acquainted with the teaching about righteousness. [14] But solid food is for the mature, who by constant use have trained themselves to distinguish good from evil. —Hebrews 5:12-14

The Bible is your fuel. It's your nourishment. Don't be thinking that you're passionate about God without being passionate about the Bible. Sooner or later (and I'm voting for sooner) you need to take a bite on your own or starve. If you chew it up the nourishment of the truth will start surging in your veins.

Nothing complicated here. You sit down at the table and you open it. Then look at it, and then read it. It doesn't take a PhD. If you're just starting out, I would suggest that you first read the Book of James. Then I would read plenty of Proverbs. Then I would suggest Paul's letter to the Ephesians. Then read some of David's Psalms. You might want to jump right into a Bible reading plan designed by someone else (we've got several suggestions at the end of this chapter). The key is getting that alone time with Jesus and the Holy Spirit at the table with the living Word. Forget being "too busy" and go for the best. Make the time and do it!

Once you're there, start off sincerely asking God to bless your time and teach you what he wants you to learn. Then, all you have to do is read and ask some key questions:

1. What does it say?
2. What does it mean?
3. How does it relate to me?
4. What do I do about it?

Under the guidance and power of the spirit you honor the word of God by honoring the things that the word of God reveals. The nice thing is that you can do all of this immediately with your children too. You don't have to have all the answers. You just have to know the questions! Start with John if you want. Find a table and just start asking the same questions with your kids that you ask yourself. Your kids will think you're brilliant! They will think you are the famous Greek philosopher Socrates. (Everybody thought he was so smart, but all he really did was sit around and ask people questions all day. That guy had it made.) If your kids start asking questions and they stick you for an answer that you don't know, just utter six magic words: "I don't know. I'll find out." Then call your pastor. That's why you pay him the big bucks.

Yeah, I know this is intimidating if you've never done it before. But there's something powerful about honoring God's word with the people that God wants you to honor. We're not just supposed to be fed. God wants us to be feeders *while* we are being fed. We do this by sharing the feast with others and modeling how they can invite others to the table and shared the feast with them too. Paul worded it this way:

> You then, my son, be strong in the grace that is in Christ Jesus. [2] And the things you have heard me say in the presence of many witnesses entrust to reliable people who will also be qualified to teach others.—2 Timothy 2:2

This is huge! God can use you as the first link in a new "spiritual food chain" that will nourish your family with the truth, and then their families, and their families for generations to come. That was the vision behind the command that God gave to the people of Israel:

These are the commands, decrees and laws the LORD your God directed me to teach you to observe in the land that you are crossing the Jordan to possess, [2] so that you, your children and their children after them may fear the LORD your God as long as you live by keeping all his decrees and commands that I give you, and so that you may enjoy long life.[3] Hear, Israel, and be careful to obey so that it may go well with you and that you may increase greatly in a land flowing with milk and honey, just as the LORD, the God of your ancestors, promised you. [4] Hear, O Israel: The LORD our God, the LORD is one. [5] Love the LORD your God with all your heart and with all your soul and with all your strength.[6] These commandments that I give you today are to be on your hearts.[7] Impress them on your children. Talk about them when you sit at home and when you walk along the road, when you lie down and when you get up. [8] Tie them as symbols on your hands and bind them on your foreheads. [9] Write them on the doorframes of your houses and on your gates. —Deuteronomy 6:6-9

When I was little, my mom took passages like this to heart. She didn't write on our doorframes, exactly, but she did pin a little 5x7 postcard about Scripture on a little corkboard by the breakfast bar in our house. (Yes, we were cool; we had the bar and bar stools and stuff). It was a picture of the rapture that had been popular back in the 70s. Pretty horrifying for a little kid actually: Planes were crashing into buildings; people were getting resurrected and ascending out of tombs; taxis were smashing into each other—fuel for nightmares for sure. I remember leaning over and looking at that thing. My mom was stirring something that the stove, and I said, "Mom, if Jesus comes back will I be going to heaven?" What followed was the most important table moment of my life. Mom sat down with me and shared from the Scriptures what it meant to be a Christian and to go to heaven.

That was a long time ago, but I remember that moment as clearly as anything. My mom understood that she could take the lead in bringing the Scriptures into our home. This understanding can break the mentalities keep us from honoring the word of God in the home.

Deuteronomy is talking about a home that is saturated with the Word of God. There's no "drive through, TV tray, potluck, pre-chewed, bar bouncing mentality in how the Bible talks about the Bible. No, it's talking about feasting on the essential nutritional truth of Scripture.

> He humbled you, causing you to hunger and then feeding you with manna, which neither you nor your ancestors had known, **to teach you that man does not live on bread alone but on every word that comes from the mouth of the** LORD...
> —Deuteronomy 8:3

ANCIENT TRUTH IN THE INFORMATION AGE

I love my old Bible. I really do. For me, nothing can replace that feel of worn leather and the smell of its yellowing pages. That thing is like a journal of my life with marks and notes all over the place. But the fact is, I'm now "old school," one of the last of the Baby Boomers from post-World War II. Our kids? They are "Gen X" and "Millennials." To them, old leather bound books look like old leather bound books. My kids are about computer games, smart phone apps and Google searches. Thankfully, God is too.

Remember, it's not the pages of the Bible that are important. It's the words of Scripture that bring life. In the digital-information age, God is opened up stunning new ways for us to experience his Words without ever even opening a paper bound book. Hundreds of apps and programs are giving us access to the truths of Scripture like never before. Yeah, you might think that computers and tablets and smart phones are distracting your kids from God, but God can use them to launch your kids into a relevant encounter with truth using the mediums they love. Let me give you three to explore:

www.YouVersion.com

This Bible app was created by my friends at LifeChurch.tv that wanted to attract younger people. They knew they needed both to be technically advanced and offer truth to people for free. Today the YouVersion of the Bible is available in 600 translations in more than 400 languages and has far surpassed 100 million downloads.

www.BlueLetterBible.org

What used to take me hours of research in a seminary library can now be accomplished in a few seconds by anyone with a pulse. Websites like www.BlueLetterBible.org give us instant access to an insane amount of research, commentaries, and study tools.

- Want to know the Greek translation of "love" in John 3:16? Click!
- Want to know the Hebrew verb tense in Deuteronomy 6:5? Click!
- What to compare four different English translations side-by-side? Click!
- Want to know what a dozen really smart guys said about Genesis 1:1? Click!

Seriously, computers have made intense Bible study so easy that those of us who grew up in the old school are pretty convinced it's cheating.

www.GloBible.

You really have to experience this one to understand how cool it is. By focusing the truth of Scripture through different "lenses" the GloBible empowers you to explore the Scriptures from multiple points of view all once. This amazing program is highly visual, interactive, and continues to morph as new versions are released. At even comes in a free "lite" version that never expires.

Honestly, if you're willing to think outside of the box of the way we used to do it, engaging the Bible with our kids has never been easier or more powerful. Never before has the truth of the Bible been served to the world like it is now. It's all you can eat, it's all free, it's 24/7/365 and your kids will eat it up... so will you.

BACK AT OUR SHARE-HOLDERS MEETING

After gathering my wife and my kids together, I shared my embarrassment and my concerns. Yes, there was a lot of really good stuff happening in our family, yet we had let the good stuff dominate the best. Cindy and I had created a very strong learning environment in our home when it came to academics. I had dropped the ball when it came to serving the truth of God's Word to my crew.

My kids were becoming masters at memorizing facts and formulas, but we weren't letting the Word of God richly dwell in our hearts or minds (Colossians 3:16) I told them if we do not choose to holistically honor the Bible, everything else in our lives will fall to subjectivity and average. Yet if we hide the Word of God in our hearts, we are less likely to sin (Psalm 119:11) and God's word will light up where we are and where we are going (Psalm 119:105).

So then, I put on my man pants and implemented a plan for mandatory reading of the Scripture. If my child wants me to pay for their phone all I ask is one verse text to me from their daily reading. No verse…no cell service. Is it legalistic? No. I make him brush their teeth. I make them look both ways before they cross the street. I make them eat their vegetables. I make them go to the doctor and get their shots. I make them do their homework. This is our responsibility as parents. We are the CEOs and COOs. We control the remote. We control the phones. We can lead them to the work of God too. I don't want my kids to think calculus is more important than the Word of God. I'm not saying academics aren't important. But when academics and athletics become the required and the Bible becomes elective, we dishonor him and his Word. So now I'm going to make them memorized God's Word—and it's not just going to be good for them, it's going to be fun for them. I'm even going to let them take ownership of the process.

The bottom line is this: God's word is the determining factor for God's best in our lives. It's the truth that brings power to parenting. If are not willing to honor this text, then everything else is going to fail. It might not ultimately bomb, but you and your kids will miss out on the best that God has to offer unless you honor the word of God. God's word is the ticket, the real deal. When you make it optional, you'll miss out on his best. God's word is passionate. Every detail is for you and for me and for our kids. It's time to bring the Bible to the table and make it a feast, because it truly is eatable.

Why is the Word the determining factor for God's best? Because it is truth *and*, ultimately, it points us to the source of all truth and life: Jesus.

> You have never heard his voice nor seen his form, [38] nor does his [the Father's]word dwell in you, for you do not believe the one he sent. [39] You study the Scriptures diligently because you think that in them you have eternal life. **These are the very Scriptures that testify about me,** [40] yet you refuse to come to me to have life. —John 5:37-40

> Taste and see that the LORD is good; blessed is the one who takes refuge in him. The lions may grow weak and hungry, but those who seek the LORD lack no good thing. —Psalm 34:8,10

God, I pray that you would give me a spirit of faithfulness to your table, just as your word teaches us. From the beginning of Genesis to the end of Revelation the table is found. God, help me to prioritize table moments in my family, in my life. God, let me feast on your Word at your table every day. I want to be serious about this deal. I want to honor you. I want to put my weight behind you, Jesus, just as you honor us and put your weight behind us through the resurrection and the redemptive work of your son on the cross. Use me to raise up my kids as the next generation that understands the importance of the table and serves the truth of your Word, and your son Jesus to the world.

Amen.

AT THE TABLE WITH JESUS

Spend some time talking with the Lord about his Word.
Read and ponder 1 Peter 2:1-9

1. What does it say?
2. What does it mean?
3. How does it relate to me?
4. What do I do about it?

Read and ponder Hebrews 5:9-14

1. What does it say?
2. What does it mean?
3. How does it relate to me?
4. What do I do about it?

[I would suggest including a personal Bible study plan that covers the essentials of the gospel and the promise of the Holy Spirit]

FOR GROUP DISCUSSION

Read Nehemiah 8, the account of Nehemiah and his team finishing the reconstruction of the walls of Jerusalem.

- Why do you think they were so grieved and then so happy?
- Have you or your group ever celebrated God's living word like that?
- Why or why not?

Talk about the dynamics in your group. In what ways does your group fall prey to these mentalities:

1. Drive-Through mentality.
2. TV tray mentality.
3. The Pot-Luck mentality
4. The Pre-chewed mentality
5. The bar-bouncing mentality.

What would it look like if your group served "pure milk" to spiritual infants? (1 Peter2)

What would it look like if you served "solid food" to more mature believers? (Hebrews 5)

[I would suggest including a plan for group Bible study that is based on the Bible and simple hermeneutics rather than a pre-prepared lessons]

AT THE TABLE WITH YOUR KIDS

Call a "family shareholders meeting." If you want to be fancy, take them out like it's a corporate dinner, or borrow actual office space from someone you know and do it around a real conference table.

Give them your report.

Point out all the stuff that's going really well.

Affirm each of them as a welcome an indispensable part of the family business.

Read Deuteronomy 6:1-9.

Have each kid pick out the thing they feel is most important in this passage.

Brainstorm about how you could apply the following commands in your home:

*⁶ These commandments that I give you today **are to be on your hearts**.*

-
-
-
-

*⁷ **Impress them** on your children.*

-
-
-
-

***Talk about them** when you sit at home and when you walk along the road, when you lie down and when you get up.*

-
-
-
-

*⁸ **Tie them as symbols** on your hands and bind them on your foreheads.*

-
-
-
-

⁹ *Write **them** on the doorframes of your houses and on your gates.*—
Deuteronomy 6

- •

- •

- •

- •

Pray for a while, ask God for his guidance, and I go back through and pick out the top ideas that can be implemented right now.

Ask God, to work through your lives by the power of the Holy Spirit to make these things a reality.

TABLE #3: MINISTRY

Leg #1: Love

For who is greater, the one who is at the table or the one who serves?

Jesus, at the table… —Luke 22:27

comforTABLE [kuhm-fer-t*uh*-b*uh*l] adjective
1. Being in a state of physical or mental comfort; contented and undisturbed; at ease.
2. Where Christians sit and get fat and lazy because they don't know what they are created for.

WE WERE JUST one more normal family in a normal neighborhood. It was a good neighborhood, normal by American standards and we fit in just fine. Mom and dad would sometimes put us on the church bus when we were little and a couple times a year, (Christmas and Easter) they would wash us and dress us up and try to keep us from fidgeting while the preacher talked and our feet stuck out straight over the edge of the pew. But that was about it. We were American, middle class and we were comfortable.

But when I was nine, somebody came into our lives who messed up our contented, undisturbed life of ease… and she did it at the table.

Mrs. Plumlee started having us over for dinner. She was an amputee with only one leg and couldn't use prosthesis much, so most of the time she was on crutches, but she was definitely walking her walk with

Christ. She would cook up this spread and lay it out and we would chow down—Norman Rockwell stuff. But there was more to it than that, much more. She was doing us a simple service and we appreciated it greatly, yet Mrs. Plumlee knew that we needed to eat something more than the meatloaf and potatoes. She used that table to invite us to drink living water, and eat the bread of life. She was really just passing on the invitation she had accepted from Jesus—so we could let him into the house and dine with him. She just kept feeding us and inviting us to come to church.

We just kept on eating, but one Sunday, we took her up on her invitation… and that changed everything.

My mom was already a Christian, but getting into church lit her fire again and she started to live for Jesus in new ways. Then, my brother got saved. Then I got saved. Then my sister prayed to receive Christ. Then I remember my dad sitting at a table with the pastor and *he* prayed to receive Christ right there at our table when he was 39. He was baptized the following Sunday.

One by one, that's how we all came to know Christ. It's crazy to think about it really. It's like we were all stacked up like a big row of dominoes ready to tumble over into a world of faith. For all I know, we could still be sitting there, stacked up and ready. It was Martha Plumlee that gave us the flick, starting the chain reaction that has transformed our lives on earth and changed the trajectory of our eternity.

Mrs. Plumlee died of cancer at the young age of 36. She could've just hung out at the comforTABLE like everybody else was doing. But instead she just tweaked what she was good at and served us at her table, so that she could invite us church, so we could accept Christ's offer to dine with him.

She didn't have to do that.

And I shudder when I think about what our lives would be like if she hadn't.

MINISTRY AT THE TABLE

When marriages are healthy and families are healthy, God's church is going to be healthy too, that's when real ministry can happen at the table. There's no doubt that the marriage is better when frequent dinner dates are on the calendar. The family is stronger when it's regularly seated around the table.

The local church is also a table, a place of ministry with food prepared— living bread and life giving water—ready to be served to guests who have been invited in as guests and offered a seat. The church is the place where the King, is served, the Bread of Life. Where Jesus, the Bread of Life, (as my mentor Pastor Ed Young Jr. says) the king of complex carbs, is placed and presented and given to those desperate for rescue. The church is the table where people must be able to come and receive spiritual sustenance to go deeper, but not only deeper in their walk with God, but a place to bring those who are desperate for rescue to find Jesus Christ in a real, in a fresh, in a beautifully presented way.

We are called not only to be fed at the table, but to feed others, and that means we need to push back, stand up and server others.

We are the body of Christ in action. He has allowed us, as the body of Christ, to make the presentation of the feast that he invites all to join. Jesus living through us so those around us can feast as well. The problem is that many of us are sitting at the comforTABLE. The church can become a place where people come not to be nourished and fueled for ministry, but to indulge and binge and get fat and lazy. That's not healthy for anybody. And it's certainly not helpful to those who are hungry outside wandering through life, desperately trying to fill the emptiness inside of them.

The greatest commands are that we would love to God with all we have and that we would love our neighbors as ourselves.

Greater love has no man than this, and that a man lays down his life for his friends.

Yes, the table is where Christ is served to the hungry. We do find our nourishment and our strength at this table continually. But that's not all. There's a time when we push back from the table and serve so we can love others as Christ loved us.

Jesus is the vine. We are the branches. If we abide in His love, we will bear much fruit... fruit that can be served to others. Jesus is the one that bears fruit through us so that those around us can feast at his table as well. *That's* what the table of ministry is all about.

- He sacrificed so we can serve.
- He fed us so we can feed.
- He loved us so we can love.

When I realized this, I was sitting at the table, with my dad, then shared with him what had happened. Over a McDonalds sausage and egg mcmuffin, I shared my call to ministry. His response, "Go be the next Billy Graham son".

That was all I needed at the table with my dad to confirm the call from my Heavenly Father. I was full and fueled up for action. It was time to let Jesus overflow.

THE "iChair"

Jesus loved the table. He ministered at the table, and the table moments that men and women shared with him transformed their lives. But it was rarely a comforTABLE. Encounters with Jesus almost always exposed the inner crud in a person's heart. With a few words, he could, shine a light into dark places of the soul, and then show them the way out if they were willing to follow him.

The Last Supper that Jesus shared with his disciples is a prime example of an encounter with Jesus at the table. There's so many facets to this one meal that you can look from different angles time after time and still see different new ways that Jesus used this "table moment" to point wayward hearts in the right direction. Here are a few excerpts from Luke's account in the 22nd chapter:

> Now the Festival of Unleavened Bread, called the Passover, was approaching, [2] and the chief priests and the teachers of the law were looking for some way to get rid of Jesus, for they were

afraid of the people...⁷Then came the day of Unleavened Bread on which the Passover lamb had to be sacrificed...¹⁴When the hour came, Jesus and his apostles reclined at the table.¹⁵And he said to them, "I have eagerly desired to eat this Passover with you before I suffer. ¹⁶For I tell you, I will not eat it again until it finds fulfillment in the kingdom of God."

Get the picture? Jesus is standing on the threshold of death. All human history is hanging in the balance. The next three days will completely transform eternity for billions of souls as he's beaten and hung from the cross in the scorching heat of the Middle Eastern sun. His best friends and closest followers were deeply concerned about what was going to happen to their leader and their teacher. They too felt the weight of the world and the suffering that lie ahead. Right? Umm, not so much:

²⁴A dispute also arose among them as to which of them was considered to be greatest.

What? Give me a break! The spiritual destiny of the human race is on the line, and these guys are wondering who is going to be bigger and better than the others?! It sounds like a couple of kids fighting on the playground, like a couple of boxers spouting off before a match, like, like... well, like a lot of us who are supposed leaders in the church. Why? These guys had become major-league comforTABLE. They were acting like a bunch of babies, really—a bunch of babies sitting in high chairs pulled up to the table demanding what they wanted.

I've had kids, and I know how kids in highchairs work. At that age, the kid really can't think of anything other than the needs he feels right there at the moment. Does he have any concern about mom or dad or the needs of anybody else around him? Nope. It's all about numero uno. *I want food! I don't want THAT food! I want my diaper changed! I want... I want... I want...*

And let me be honest here, because there are plenty of people in highchairs around the table of ministry that think and feel the same way. I know, they don't sit in *real* highchairs like babies; they sit in what I call the *iChair*:

"I want the King James version!"
"I want more contemporary music!"
"I want more hymns!"
"I want shorter sermons!"
"I want some recognition!"
"I want... I want... I want...!"

There are a lot of us the sitting in the iChair around the table of marriage claiming our rights instead of accepting our biblical responsibility.

"I want dinner."
"I want my clothes ironed."
"I want a weekend with my girlfriends."
And there are a lot of the sitting in the iChair as parents.
"I wish you were more like Johnny down the street."
"I wish your grades were like your sisters."
"I wish you listened."

It was obvious that the disciples were sitting in iChairs at the last supper. Jesus cut through the junk and exposed them right there at the table during dinner... and he used the table as an example:

> [25] Jesus said to them, "The kings of the Gentiles lord it over them; and those who exercise authority over them call themselves Benefactors. [26] But you are not to be like that. Instead, the greatest among you should be like the youngest, and the one who rules like the one who serves. [27] For who is greater, the one who is at the table or the one who serves? Is it not the one who is at the table? But I am among you as one who serves.—Luke 22:25-27

The power of this table moment can hardly be over emphasized. I mean, get a handle on the situation: Jesus is ready to go to the cross, and they are whining like a couple of kids about who gets to bat first at recess. Yes, he said, in the world kings rule. At most tables, the one sitting *is* greater than the one who serves. *"But you are not to be like that..."*

All of a sudden, this dinner became very *un*comforTABLE. When you sit in the iChair, it's all about *you* when it's really all about *him*, and it's really all about *service*. Jesus didn't just correct them with words, he took action, showing them how to grow up and get out of the iChair.

PUSHING BACK

² The evening meal was in progress, and the devil had already prompted Judas, the son of Simon Iscariot, to betray Jesus. ³ Jesus knew that the Father had put all things under his power, and that he had come from God and was returning to God; ⁴ so he got up from the meal, took off his outer clothing, and wrapped a towel around his waist. ⁵ After that, he poured water into a basin and began to wash his disciples' feet, drying them with the towel that was wrapped around him...

> ¹²When he had finished washing their feet, he put on his clothes and returned to his place. "Do you understand what I have done for you?" he asked them. ¹³"You call me 'Teacher' and 'Lord,' and rightly so, for that is what I am. ¹⁴Now that I, your Lord and Teacher, have washed your feet, you also should wash one another's feet. ¹⁵I have set you an example that you should do as I have done for you. ¹⁶Very truly I tell you, no servant is greater than his master, nor is a messenger greater than the one who sent him. ¹⁷Now that you know these things, you will be blessed if you do them.--John 13:2-5, 12-17

Imagine, for a moment, you were one of the disciples and that night. Seriously, close your eyes and vividly imagine sitting at the table. Smell the food. See the dim light that came through the windows and from the candles... and imagine yourself entering into the debate about who was the "greatest".

We have to give the disciples a little bit of slack here, because even though they had read the prophecies, and even though Jesus had spoken clearly about his coming death, they really didn't get it. But we really can't give ourselves any slack here, because we know the rest of the story and can look back and see everything that was going on in that room. Jesus died for us, was resurrected for us, and now his spirit lives inside of us, guiding us through his complete eternal words in the Bible. I think you can say that we are truly without excuse. And yet, don't we all, in some ways, still find ourselves sitting in the iChair?

My friends, as a member of God's church, rather than just sitting constantly and taking in the food, at some point you have to grow up and, as Ed Young Jr. said, "push back from the table." We will forever draw our nourishment from Christ, so in a sense we never leave the table ourselves, but like Jesus, at some point, it's time to get up from the table, wrap a towel around our waist, and serve in a spirit of love.

DOING IT

When the Bible says of the greatest commandment is to love God and to love others, it is not talking about a feeling. Love *does* stuff. Love *serves*. Getting out of the iChair and wrapping the towel around our waist, and washing feet is the *real* deal of discipleship. Why? Because every time we do this, something eternal is taking place.

> [34]Then he called the crowd to him along with his disciples and said: "Whoever wants to be my disciple must deny themselves and take up their cross and follow me. [35] For whoever wants to save their life will lose it, but whoever loses their life for me and for the gospel will save it. [36] What good is it for someone to gain the whole world, yet forfeit their soul? Mark 8:34-36

- From Mrs. Plumlee, love looked like an evening meal at the table for her neighbors (when, I'm sure, she would have rather just sat down and rested her one good leg.)
- Invite a needy friend.
- Bring in someone who needs marital encouragement.
- Open the door at the cafe during Sunday service.
- Love on a child in a preschool room with some Goldfish crackers.

Now, if you're not careful this can start to sound like a whole bunch of do's and don'ts. But remember, love is And let me tell you, Christians are great at creating lists of laws that they use to help judge people and categorize them into those who are spiritual or unspiritual, committed or casual. But that's really not the point at all. When we accepted Jesus' invitation to come in and dine, he *really* came in. A very powerful and practical spiritual exchange took place that freed us up from legalistic standards of behavior and performance. Paul was a very accomplished *self*-righteous leader. But after he started dining with Jesus, he knew that his righteousness came *from* Christ who was *in* him and had died *for* him.

> [19] "For through the law I died to the law so that I might live for God. [20] I have been crucified with Christ and I no longer live, but Christ lives in me. The life I now live in the body, I live by faith in the Son of God, who loved me and gave himself for me. [21] I do not set aside the grace of God, for if righteousness could be gained through the law, Christ died for nothing!" Galatians 2:19-21

You are free to live and to love and to serve in any way that Christ chooses to do so through you. And that might look very different than what anybody else thinks you should do, because Jesus, who lives inside of you, has a way of doing things different than anyone else would expect.

Back in the church I grew up in, a picture of Jesus hung on the walls of the Sunday school rooms. He was a really nice-looking guy.

His hair was well combed. His skin was smooth and slightly pale, and his eyes were gently looking up toward heaven. I'm fairly sure that picture of Jesus isn't accurate at all. First of all, Jesus was a carpenter. None of the carpenters I know look like that picture... at all. His skin would've been tanned and his hands would've been calloused and he would've had some pretty nasty biceps after lifting beams and boards all day long. What we do know for sure from Scripture is that he was a renegade and a rebel. He loved and he served in the face of hatred and selfishness. He taught this love to his disciples in his words and deeds and he lived it consistently all his days. And then, the night before he was crucified, he showed them and called them one more time to be servants and the table of ministry. Because true disciples get out of the iChair. True disciples love. True disciples serve.

Dear Lord (and I mean that, you are my Lord),

I don't want to sit at the comforTABLE. I want to serve at a table of ministry that is loving and serving the people around us. Lord, you are the greatest. By the power of your spirit in me, I want to live as you live, as a living sacrifice of love. Teach me to serve. Keep me always listening to your leading, and searching the truth of your Scriptures, so that I can hear your special calling to me to push back from the table so that you love others through me as you desire.

Amen.

AT THE TABLE WITH JESUS

Read.
- Ponder Luke 22:1-26-- but do more than just read it. Imagine yourself in that situation as if Jesus were speaking directly to you (because he really is).

Pour out heart.
- Ask the spirit to search your heart and show you your ways. Ask him to truly reveal specific examples of things you

think, feel, and to that are related to this beautiful passage of Scripture.

Listen.

- Write down significant things that God reveals to you through his word and through his spirit.
- Ask him to show you the general areas where he has gifted you and equipped you to serve and love others.
- Ask him to show you one thing that he wants you to do in the next day, to love and serve someone else.

AT THE TABLE WITH YOUR "TEAM"

Everybody has a "team", whether it's at church, at work, or your spouse, or your family, or maybe even an official team through your ministry organization or church. Bring this team to a table.

- Share with them what you have been learning so far through the book.
- Turn on some background worship music
- Read John 13:1-17, explain to your team why they are so important to you, and that you want to serve them as Christ commanded.
- Have some towels and of tubs of warm soapy water available. One by one, actually wash the feet of the people at your table of ministry. Take the lead. Leaders serve. Don't be surprised if others follow into the same to you and each other.
- When you're done, pray together through John 13 and Luke 22. Pick out specific lines from these passages and ask God to make them a reality on your team.
- Ask Jesus to begin to guide you, right now, as a group, into specific facts of loving service.
- Make a plan to get started!

FOR GROUP DISCUSSION

- Skim back through this chapter and circle any principles or ideas that look completely opposite of the way things tend to look in the world. Share those things with each other.

- Share a time when you received awesome service from someone at a table.

  How did it make you feel?

  Did you feel like doing the same for others? Or were you comfortable just taking it in? Be honest!

- Share a time when you received really lousy service from someone at a table.

  How did that make you feel? How did you respond? How does your response reveal your expectations about being served?

- Talk about different ways you struggle to get out of the iChair.
- As a group, what opportunities are there right now to love someone through sacrificial service?

  What's holding you back from doing it?

Table 3: Ministry

Leg #2: Creativity

For we are God's handiwork, created in Christ Jesus to do good works, which God prepared in advance for us to do.

—Ephesians 2:10

pivoTABLE [piv-*uh*-tabl] *adjective*
1. Of, pertaining to, or serving as a <u>pivot</u>. Of vital or critical importance: *a pivotal event.*
2. The radical change in direction that takes place when someone realizes they are created to be creatively excellent.

God is a creative God. He knows how to start with nothing and make everything. And he knows how to take stuff that is dead and bring it back to life. He knows how to make all things beautiful in his time and how to make all things work together for good. He's in the business of taking "normal" stuff and transforming it into supernatural stuff—stuff that brings him glory on earth and in eternity.

Listen, when you open the door of your life to Christ and accepted his invitation to dine together at the table, everything shifted. Paul says that you became a "new creature." That means God created you uniquely to be a reflection of his image. I'm telling you, don't settle for normal. You've been born again for a purpose: To enjoy Christ at the table and serve others there creatively.

Do you get it? You have been created to be part of a creative team that is serving Jesus Christ to the world. This is a pivoTABLE principle. If you get it, God can use this realization to rotate your life in a new direction, he can use it as a tipping point that can launch you into new areas of service, and when you join with others who understands this pivoTABLE principle of creativity, God can use you to leverage global impact in ways that you could never accomplish by yourself.

THE FOOD OF JESUS

John chapter 4 records an amazing encounter that Jesus had with a woman of the world and his disciples. Jesus was always ministering creatively "outside of the box" and this passage reflects the passion that Jesus had for the table, how he viewed the table, and his constant creativity and inviting others to come to drink and feast with him at the table. That was the invitation he gave the wayward Samaritan women at the well—it was a definite "table moment" of transformation, but just afterward, the focus of Jesus' disciples shifted:

> [31] Meanwhile his disciples urged him, "Rabbi, eat something." [32] But he said to them, "I have food to eat that you know nothing about." [33] Then his disciples said to each other, "Could someone have brought him food?"

Interesting! They are in the heat of ministry, but his disciples *urged* Jesus away from serving others so that he could get his own needs met. It's almost like they're trying to get him to get in the iChair. Jesus stayed focused, however and came back at them with words that reverberate with the true spirit of ministry at the table:

> [34] "My food," said Jesus, "is to do the will of him who sent me and to finish his work.

Bam! That's pivoTABLE, isn't it? They want him to eat to live, but he lets them know that he's living for something else: the will and work of God.

God's will and God's work were his fuel, but that's not all. The work Jesus did was not normal. In fact, he broke the norms with bold creativity. He was so far off the charts on the creativity scale that his guys didn't know what to think.

- He broke the norms of gender by ministering to a woman.

- He broke the norms of cultural by ministering to a Samaritan
- He broke the norms of society by ministering a lost soul who was the least in her community (By the sounds of it, she had slept with half the guys in the village.).

There's a lot more to this story than just those points, and you'll get a chance to dig into that story yourself at the end of this chapter, but let's just say that Jesus' willingness to be creative in this situation raised plenty of eyebrows.

> [27] Just then his disciples returned and were surprised to find him talking with a woman. But no one asked, "What do you want?" or "Why are you talking with her?"[28] Then, leaving her water jar, the woman went back to the town and said to the people, [29] "Come, see a man who told me everything I ever did. Then something amazing happened. Even though the revelation (that Jesus knew everything this woman had done) probably scared the bejesus out of every guy in town, people started coming to Jesus. Could this be the Messiah?" [30] They came out of the town and made their way toward him.[39] Many of the Samaritans from that town believed in him because of the woman's testimony, "He told me everything I ever did." –John 4:27-30

Again, there is tons of stuff to learn from this chapter, but the two principles I'm focusing on right now are the pivotable ones:

1) Jesus had pushed back from the table so that he could serve others and refused to get back in the iChair.
2) His "food" was doing the work of God... and that work was intensely, out-of-the-box creative.

YOUR FOOD

A lot of sincere believers look at the table of ministry and feel a sense of drudgery, obligation, and self-denial. Those feelings are just flat out wrong. That perception of service and love is a lie of Satan. He uses those feelings to rob us of joy and to drain our ministry of passion. When those lies take root, we believe that ministry forces us to do something that we don't want to do and to be someone that we are not. Nothing could be further from the truth.

> For it is by grace you have been saved, through faith—and this is not from yourselves, it is the gift of God— not by works, so that no one can boast.[10] For we are God's handiwork, created in Christ Jesus to do good works, which God prepared in advance for us to do.—Ephesians 2:8-9

In order for our creativity to be unleashed *in ministry*, we first have to grasp the fact that God's creativity is first unleashed *in us*. It's not by *our* works; we are *his* "handiwork, created in Christ Jesus" do the things that he created "in advance for us to do." That's a complete paradigm shift! When we get out of the iChair and then come back to the table to love and serve creatively, this pivoTABLE truth can unleash incredible creativity.

He created each of us to be creative in a ministry that he has already created us to be a part of. You can't get much more creative than that.

So the key is not to become somebody that you aren't in order to do things that you don't want to do. The key to unleashing creativity is to discover who he has already made you to be, so that he can love and serve others through you as he already created you to do.

Who are you in Christ?

- **You are new creature.**
- **You are forgiven.**
- **You are clean.**
- **You're a Temple of the Holy Spirit who is in you.**
- **You have the mind of Christ.**
- **You are a child of God.**
- **You are the head not the tail.**

- **You are blessed in the country and blessed in the city.**
- **You blessed going in and blessed going out.**
- **Your kids are blessed**
- **Your investments are blessed.**
- **You will always be on top and never on bottom.**
- **You are surrounded with favor.**

The whole Bible gives you truth after truth about who you are in black and white. You've also been given unique skills, gives and the personality that "fits" within the body of Christ so that you can creatively to what he has created you to do best and to do it with the most joy.

When you get alone with Jesus at the table at the end of this chapter, you'll talk with Jesus about this and then listen so he can confirm the specific ways that he has created you. But for now, go back and read those verses in Ephesians chapter 2 just one more time. Let your soul soak it in!

TEAMS WITH CREATIVE EXCELLENCE

Back in John chapter 4, when Jesus told the disciples that his food was to do the will of God, I really don't think the disciples got it. Yeah, the information probably got stored somewhere in their brains, but they didn't get it in their heart… until after the resurrection. When the Holy Spirit came into those guys' lives, everything changed. It started in their hearts, and then it leaked its way out into everything they did, and they did a lot. The Apostle Paul picked up on it for sure. And when he got it, he saw how all of us were created to work together as a body:

> Therefore if you have any encouragement from being united with Christ, if any comfort from his love, if any common sharing in the Spirit, if any tenderness and compassion, [2] then make my joy complete by being like-minded, having the same love, being one in spirit and of one mind. [3] Do nothing out of selfish ambition or vain conceit. Rather, in humility value others above yourselves, [4] not looking to your own interests but each of you to the interests

of the others… [12] Therefore, my dear friends, as you have always obeyed—not only in my presence, but now much more in my absence—continue to work out your salvation with fear and trembling, [13] for it is God who works in you to will and to act in order to fulfill his good purpose.—Philippians 2:1-4, 12-13

Notice two key phrases in the last sentence of that passage: Something works in you "to will" and "to act" to fulfill the purposes of God. In other words, you have to *want* it and *do* it. But who does the work? God does. He is the one "who works in you." He created us. Now he creates through us. The key is not trying to do anything creative in our own strength, but allowing God to work through us so that he "wills" it and "does" it.

This unleashes the creative excellence of God to work through us.

> Whatever you do, work at it with all your heart, as working for the Lord, not for human masters, [2]since you know that you will receive an inheritance from the Lord as a reward. It is the Lord Christ you are serving. Colossians 3:23-24

Remember, we're not just serving him, but we are serving him to others. Jesus is the ultimate food. He is the King of the complex carbs, the Bread of Life, the Living Water. We should be presenting this ultimate food with creative excellence! I don't believe that the church should present Jesus like food that is dished out at a weenie roast. He should be presented with all of the pride and care that a fine, five course meal is place on a table.

If you're doing something meaningful around the table of your home, you don't use paper plates. You bring out the china. Why do we settle for "cheap" in ministry? You never see Styrofoam cups at our church. Styrofoam says, "Hey we got these at the Moose Lodge we hope you're happy with it." No offence to the Moose Lodge, but we put the best out every Sunday; because we have got offer our best when we are presenting the gospel message of Jesus Christ. It's must be excellent because lives are at stake. Our focus is not the "already-fed." We don't exist to make believers fat and lazy. Our focus is to Share The Word…Reach The World.

We expect those who are already full to get out of the iChair and start serving around the table, rather than being "guests" at it. We have the privilege of being able to dine with guests who are desperate for eternal life change, who show true repentance, and who experience Jesus for the first time in a real way.

We focus on our strengths, compensate for weaknesses, and to what we know we can do well. Nothing more. Nothing less. A good restaurant doesn't have a 95 item menu. Because they would end up doing 95 average choices. A good restaurant has about 15 things on the menu. They know they can only do some things well so the smart ones will do those things with creative excellence.

When Cindy and I were in the Dallas area, we went to an Asian grill. Their menu was one side of one piece of paper. And it was unbelievably good. My guess is that if they tried to serve spaghetti, it would've been horrible. They stuck with what they knew they were created to cook and it rocked. It's the same way as a church. We're not going to try to be like every other church in everywhere else. We've got a table to present and not every restaurant is going to be the same.

Don't worry, you're not alone. He's placed you on a carefully selected team, just like the cooks and waiters and hosts and janitors at (name of favorite restaurant) and all you have to do is what he created you to do as part of the Church that is creatively serving Christ to the world. Remember, you don't have to do it all. In fact, you don't have to do it at all. It is God who is at work in us to fulfill his good purposes.

When he starts to move through you and your team, he is likely to do it in creative ways that most people would never even imagine. God is a creative God. Look at the Bible!

How about the story of Jonah? That is creativity at its finest! I mean, come on! The guy disobeyed. God said, "Go this way to Tarsus." Jonah checked his GPS and went 180° in the opposite direction. He got on a boat, and a major storm started to blow. The waves were rising, people were getting panicky and they were chucking off cargo. They were like, "Who is the reason for this?" That's when we see the leg of creativity in God's table of ministry. Jonah says, "I'm a Hebrew" and tells the shipmates, "Chuck me over and this thing will calm down." So they gave him the toss as Jonah thanked God it wasn't Shark Week on Discovery Channel. A huge fish swallowed him whole. Jonah repented and he was regurgitated onto dry land of Nineveh, the largest metropolitan in the area. He preached and people repented—lots of them! Why? Because he was an unusually gifted speaker? No, it's because he smelled like puke and he was bleached white! (Maybe not, but still, I think that'd be fun.) I mean, vomit a guy up on the beach? That's creative! Look at the picture God made here. He was showing the resurrection, the death, burial, and resurrection of Jesus Christ through a fish! *Three days. Three days in the belly, resurrected again to preach the gospel.* That's a creative God.

What about Sodom and Gomorrah? That's a leg of creativity, isn't it? Lot and his family were running for their lives before God's judgment fell upon a horribly sinful city. Just like we are told to run from sin, God commanded lot to move! Run! Get out of there and don't look back! Lot obeyed. But Lots wife looked back (just like some people return to sin.) What did God do? Turned her into a pillar of salt! I mean, God could have done anything. He could have zapped her with lightening, could have opened a hole for her to fall in, or he could have had her just keel over, symbolizing the way that sin leads to death. But noooooo. He turns her into a pillar of salt...why? God wants us to stop looking back. When we keep looking back at our old life we "stockpile" our effectiveness at being the salt of the earth. That's a good one.

How about Daniel in the lion's den? This guy should have been the evening meal, but instead, God shut the mouth of every lion in that hole, and Daniel lived to pray another day.

Or Shadrach, Meshach, and Abednego? I mean, God gave them some of the most creative names in the Bible, but then he stopped them from getting cooked in a fiery furnace. God's creativity just goes and goes. He tells a guy to rub mud on his eyes to heal his blindness. It works. He takes five loaves and two fish from a boy and feeds thousands. He created things like rainbows, DNA and the duckbilled platypus. The list goes on and on...

Yet, more than all other things he did, God showed his creativity when he, the creator of man became a man himself, walked on the earth he had made, died for our sins on a tree he created, so he could re-create us and empower us to tell the story to others as creatively as possible. That's what his creativity means to us, and that's the legacy of creativity we are a part of.

> [3] I thank my God every time I remember you. [4] In all my prayers for all of you, I always pray with joy [5] because of your partnership in the gospel from the first day until now, [6] being confident of this, that he who began a good work in you will carry it on to completion until the day of Christ Jesus.—Philippians 1:3-5

That's how pivoTABLE creativity really is. It's unleashing the creative power of our Creator to live through us in creative ways moment by moment to share the story. If you understand this leg of the table of ministry, if you work together as a team to serve Jesus to your community and your world at the table, people are going to hear about it and come, just like the villagers in John 4, just like I keep going back to (name of my favorite restaurant,) where the steak sizzles and the potatoes are always smooth and creamy…

Only you will be serving something eternally more significant: the bread of life and living water that satisfies like no earthly meal ever could.

Lord Jesus, I thank you and I praise you that you are in my life! I thank you that together with my brothers and sisters in you, we makeup of the body, a team, an eternal force for good that is serving up your love and your truth with excellence. Give us outrageous creativity and freedom at the table of ministry. You began a good work in us, and we believe that you will carry it on through us until the day you return. Glory to you Lord!

AT THE TABLE WITH JESUS

Read.
- Spend some time carefully reading Ephesians 2.

- Go back through this chapter with a highlighter or a pen and note specific truths about who you are in Christ.
- Pick out four truths that impact you in the most powerful way. Write them in your own words and in the first person

Pour out heart.
- Read Colossians 3:23- 24.
- Ask God to unleash this type of focused creativity through you.

Listen.

Ask God to give you truthful answers to the following questions:

- What are my skills?
- What am I good at?
- What do I really like to do?

How do you think God wants to unleash his creativity in you?
- Today:
- This week:
- This year:
- This life:

Lift these things up to the Lord in prayer. All you really need to know right now is the next step. If you follow his leading moment by moment, he will direct you along the path he has created you to travel. Be ready for things to shift; That's what it means to be pivoTABLE.

... and whatever you do, do it for the glory of God!

AT THE TABLE WITH YOUR TEAM

- Read John 4.
- Notice how food and water is a main subject. Do you think that's a coincidence or does it mean something?

- Make a long list of the intensely creative things that Jesus did in his encounter with the woman.
- How does Jesus example challenge your team to minister differently to all people in your community?
- Identify something that you already to good. How could you make it creatively excellent?
- Brainstorm together as a team on how you could bring this type of creativity and focus to all of your teams efforts to minister to your community and the world.
- Read Philippians 1:1-6 and claim his promises as your own.

FOR GROUP DISCUSSION

Skim back over this chapter, highlighting or underlining the things that jumped out to most.

- Anything new?
- Anything that grabbed you as really significant?
- Anything specific and new new he wants to do through you?

Ponder Ephesians 2:8-9 and Philippians 2:12-13

- Do you see any apparent contradictions between these verses?
- How could these verses speak as one?

What is the most important principle that you want to take away from this chapter?

Are there any specific things that are tempting you to get back into the iChair rather than allowing Christ to serve through you at the table in this way?

Table 3: Ministry

Leg #3: Community

> At the time of the banquet he sent his servant to tell those who had been invited, 'Come, for everything is now ready'… "Then the master told his servant, 'Go out to the roads and country lanes and compel them to come in, so that my house will be full.'"

> —Luke 14:17,23

insurmounTABLE (in-sur-moun-t*ah*-b*uh*l] *adjective*
1. cannot be overcome.
2. What happens at the table when the church builds community to change lives.

A pastor at a luncheon once said, "Working for a church would be an awesome job… if you didn't have to deal with people all the time." Everybody laughed. Yeah, churches are pretty cool places. It's the people that mess them up. The only problem with that line of thinking is that according to the Bible, the "church" *is* people. It wasn't until about 325 A.D. that Christians started calling buildings "church". Up to that point, it was *all* about the people—people in *community*. Check out Acts chapter 2:

44 All the believers were together and had everything in common. 45 They sold property and possessions to give to anyone who had need. 46 Every day they continued to meet together in the temple courts. And the Lord added to their number daily those who were being saved.

I just love that description of the ancient church community, and there's so much we can learn from them about building a modern church community of believers. Yes, every modern ministry needs love and a healthy dose of God's creativity.

But the table of ministry can't stand without "community" because, the church *is* community.

If we're serious about ministry, we have to be serious about building community and relationships. That's how Jesus did it. And that's how they did it in the book of Acts. They didn't just get dressed up and go to a building an hour or two a week and call it good. Those people shared *life*. They shared their time, they shared their stuff, they shared their food… because that's what a church is and that's what the church does. It's constant community.

People ask me all the time, "Shannon, how come your friends are always people that are close-knit to you within the church?" Well, for starters, I love hanging out with people that are on the same team as I am. I love hanging out with people that are passionate about Jesus. They don't necessarily have to go to the same church *building*, but they're part of the church *community*.

I see the church community as a table where Jesus (the bread of life and the living water) is served to the world. When we get our rears out of the iChair and start to love and serve in creativity as we were created to, something amazing happens: The table itself expands as the community grows. I call it "adding a leaf."

Most dining room tables are expandable. You flip a couple latches, pull it apart and add a leaf so that more people can join in the feast. That's the way I see ministry working. The community of Christ is an organism intended to grow and YOU are a crucial part.

When the fire of ministry gets ignited at the table, the community becomes combustibles.

The flames grow in intensity as soul after soul joins the feast and the table expands again and again. I've discovered that even a dinky, little church in the middle of nowhere Arkansas can send sparks that ignite the fire ministry at the furthest corners of the globe, setting the world ablaze. That's the way it worked back in the day, "the Lord added to their number daily those who were being saved." And that's the way, by God's grace, it can still work today.

ADDING A LEAF AT HOME

I believe that God can use tables wherever they might exist. A picnic table in the park, a conference table in an office building, the back booth at your favorite restaurant... Yeah, they are all places where community can be built. But there's something special about that dining room table in the middle of your home.

> They broke bread in their homes and ate together with glad and sincere hearts, praising God and enjoying the favor of all the people. —Acts 2:46-47

When you sit down at this table, you can look across and make eye to eye, heart-to-heart contact. There are very few places in the world where you can do that with someone. Breaking bread around the table shows commitment, loyalty graciousness, and gratefulness. We aren't talking about some bar where emotional disconnect takes place, where people are side-by-side. We are talking about community, beautiful community, the third leg of ministry upon which you invest and pour into others by sharing life. So if someone asks you what you are having for dinner, I think the best thing you can say is "Guests!"

It's time to "add a leaf" to your table. You probably have one gathering dust in the garage. It's time to dust that sucker off and pop that dude on the table. It's one of the most simple, powerful things that we can do in ministry. We build community when we add a leaf, making room for people in our lives, in our homes, and in our hearts. The Plumlees' "added a leaf" when opened their home and crammed us all in around the dinner table. It changed the eternal destiny of my family. Their hospitality should make we want to do the same for others, right?

Not so much. Sometimes I don't want guests at my table. Every weekend we're entertaining guests. Honestly, I think God gives some people the gift of "hospitality," but he sure didn't give it to me. I'd much rather take them out to dinner and pay the bill. It's work when you bring guests into your home. And if your wife's like my wife she prepares 48 hours in advance, because *every* room needs to be ready, just in case somebody gets lost and wanders. I'm like, "We ain't eating in here!" Cindy is like, "Here's the vacuum and toilet bowl cleaner. Gitt'er done."

Selfishly, there's something inside of *me* that wants to keep *my* house *my* house. It's supposed to be *my* space where *I* can relax, leave *my* stuff on the table and cruise around in *my* boxer shorts if *I* want. Hey, *I* work hard all week. And when *I* come home after church on a Sunday, *I* want to build a kick off my shoes, grab the newspaper, and plopped down in *my* Lazy Boy iChair.

Don't get me wrong. I'm all about boundaries. We *do* need our own space. We *do* need our own time. We *do* need meals around the table with just our family with the phones turned off and the doors locked. I'm not talking about opening a bed and breakfast or letting your house turn into a Grand Central Station where everybody and their dog can walk in, open the fridge and plopped down on the couch and start flicking through channels with your remote.

What I am talking about is community. I'm talking about adding a leaf to your dining room table on a regular basis so that you can share the bread of life and the living water with others. Honestly, "adding a leaf" in your home is going to be one of the most fulfilling, entertaining, and natural aspects of ministry with friends, neighbors and co-workers. Most towns and cities are now home for a vast assortment of immigrants and students from other countries. Some of these countries are "closed" to the gospel. Most of these immigrants and students feel lonely and isolated. They would love to be welcomed into your home.

Don't make a big deal out of it. Just share life with people. Since Jesus is your life, you'll be sharing him with others just by being together at the table.

ADDING A LEAF AT CHURCH

Sometimes people don't want their churches to grow because they want things to stay simple. I get that. And sometimes, they don't want to see their community grow because they really like their community the way it is. When things are small they are easy to manage. When it gets big it gets a little bit crazy and you have to be more strategic. If your church community is going to grow, it's a little bit more complicated than simply "adding a leaf" to a dining room table. But that's really what you're doing. You're making more room at the table so that you can serve more people. That's what happened to the early church in Acts chapter 6:

> In those days when the number of disciples was increasing, the Hellenistic Jews among them complained against the Hebraic Jews because their widows were being overlooked in the daily distribution of food. ² So the Twelve gathered all the disciples together and said, "It would not be right for us to neglect the ministry of the word of God in order to wait on tables. ³ Brothers and sisters, choose seven men from among you who are known to be full of the Spirit and wisdom. We will turn this responsibility over to them ⁴ and will give our attention to prayer and the ministry of the word."

Each of us can help "add a leaf" and build God's community when we get up from the table and start to serve at our local congregation. There are probably a bunch of official jobs that need to be filled by willing servants. But I've found that adding a leaf is more of an attitude than it is a position. Stand up and take up the towel and start loving on people in any way that you can. "Come on, take my seat. Here let me push it up for you. Can I help you? Can I serve you? Can I get you something to drink? Can I help you with this? Can I lead you in any way? Can I open a door for you? Can I help with your baby? Can I help you out of your car? Here, you just sit here, you relax, I'm gonna eat later today. I ate this morning..." That's what a servant's heart sounds like. And anybody can do it. And everybody should do it.

My son KJ came home from second grade on day and said, "Dad, my buddy Zack at PE has the coolest shoes ever. His toes stick out! I wanna cut the ends off my new shoes too." I said I'd pray about it (and did so for about .0037 seconds.) "No," I said. "That's crazy. Boy, you're not going to be cutting up a brand new pair of shoes! We paid good money bla bla bla..." I was pretty sure that my little lecture was the end of it, but KJ came back another day and asked again, "Dad, I wanna cut the ends off of my new PE shoes like my friend Zack." I rolled my eyes and said "no!" again, but as I was sitting there at home, the Spirit started tugging on my heart. *That kid doesn't have any gym shoes that fit him.* It hit me like a ton of brick. I promised KJ I would check things out with the school counselor to see what was up. They wouldn't tell me anything specific about Zack, but they did let me know that there were *a lot* of kids in that school that could use a good pair shoes.

So I went back to KJ and said "Son, we need to get your friend a good pair shoes." He got all seven-year-old-excited. The next morning, before I knew what was happening, KJ stuffed *his* new shoes in his backpack to give to his buddy. Man, I was so convicted. The Spirit kept leading. *We need a place for needy and hurting and poor to be able to go and not feel needy and hurting and poor.* My staff caught the vision and started to run with it. What emerged was "Mercy Malls," a place where people in can come and declare their need and get empowered. We treat them like kings and queens and serve them dignity. Like everything else at our church, it started small but now we are serving hundreds of families per month in four different Mercy Malls at four different campuses.

Mercy Malls is ministry in its purest form and it has created the greatest community we have ever had. It's an amazing "come to the table moment" for our community. God is *literally* filling empty stomachs and hearts at the table. We've handed it off to volunteers who run the whole thing. One of the "malls" is over 10,000 ft.^{2}! We are giving away thousands of pounds of food every month, all because my seven year old ignited the "vision of the tennis shoes," and I listened to his lead.

The church is the church when we are marching to the national anthem of God by meeting the needs of the poor. When the early church community expanded, they also created official slots that needed to be filled. Widowed women were going hungry, and so they went the extra mile to be very careful in whom they chose to "wait on tables."

I love the way that they took such care and placed such importance to fill a seemingly insignificant slot. I mean, these guys are the equivalent of busboys and waiters. Right? The leaders dumped this grunt work on the little guys so that they could do the "really important stuff." Right? Wrong. They knew how important it was that the tables were taken care of and the people sitting at those tables were loved and served properly.

So the picked the best they had, and when Stephen and his team got their act together, the result was truly combusTABLE.

> [7] So the word of God spread. The number of disciples in Jerusalem increased rapidly, and a large number of priests became obedient to the faith. —Acts 2:7

- The next time you are at your local congregation, look around and take initiative to serve and love without even being asked. Pray about it! God will show you those he wants to add to the community.
- Ask your leadership where they think you can serve the most. They will know the needs, and hopefully they will know you well enough to know what would be a good fit.
- Don't have a come and get it mentality, have a food truck mentality...go where they are hungry.

Listen, this is a big deal. It's not just about you, it's about the world. When people start serving at the table as a way of life on a regular basis with a team of other like-minded servants, the table not only grows, but new tables of community can be built to serve Jesus in new cities. This is actually happening all over the place. Some are calling it "the multi-site church revolution." Rather than just growing and growing, churches are dividing and dividing by sending people and resources to new communities where the process starts all over again. Some people call them "satellite churches" that orbit around the mother ship. We just say that we have different "campuses" of the same community. It doesn't matter what the words are, but the principle is powerful: When a church community is combusTABLE it's not just flammable, it can be explosive, sending sparks all over the place.

By his grace, God has used Brand New Church to create church communities in 7 locations as well as our iCampus, which is reaching hundreds of people each week. A couple of years ago, I wrote a book called *Transforming Church in Rural America: Breaking all the Rurals.* God got it into the right hands. People who read that book and wanted to apply the insurmounTABLE principles started our last several campuses.

Listen; when you're ready to serve, anything can happen. God works through service. When a servant opens his heart God can move in and start to move. That's a simple principle that any church can use and, by God's grace, add a leaf again and again as their community of faith grows and grows. We've got another campus coming, and we have another campus coming after that. It's not about getting bigger and bigger. It's about multiplying. I believe in 10 years God's is going to give us 100 campuses that average 50+-- that's 5,000 people that are going be able to sit at the table, all because the people of our church have caught the vision for "adding a leaf" at the table.

The account of Stephen and the early church, however, is far more than a simple model for good church organization and delegation. Stephen, a lowly busboy and waiter, shows the power of one who serves at the table, and the ultimate sacrifice that may be required.

> Now Stephen, a man full of God's grace and power, performed great wonders and signs among the people. [9] Opposition arose, however, from members of the Synagogue of the Freedmen (as it was called)—Jews of Cyrene and Alexandria as well as the provinces of Cilicia and Asia—who began to argue with Stephen. [10] But they could not stand up against the wisdom the Spirit gave him as he spoke…

> [51] "You stiff-necked people! Your hearts and ears are still uncircumcised. You are just like your ancestors: You always resist the Holy Spirit! [52] Was there ever a prophet your ancestors did not persecute? They even killed those who predicted the coming of the Righteous One. And now you have betrayed and murdered him— [53] you who have received the law that was given through angels but have not obeyed it."

> [54] When the members of the Sanhedrin heard this, they were furious and gnashed their teeth at him. [55] But Stephen, full of

the Holy Spirit, looked up to heaven and saw the glory of God, and Jesus standing at the right hand of God. [56]"Look," he said, "I see heaven open and the Son of Man standing at the right hand of God."

[57]At this they covered their ears and, yelling at the top of their voices, they all rushed at him, [58]dragged him out of the city and began to stone him. Meanwhile, the witnesses laid their coats at the feet of a young man named Saul.

[59]While they were stoning him, Stephen prayed, "Lord Jesus, receive my spirit." [60]Then he fell on his knees and cried out, "Lord, do not hold this sin against them." When he had said this, he fell asleep. —Acts 8:8-10, 52-60

Get this: We don't need another small community church. We need to serve Jesus in a way that draws a community to church. That type of service requires tough choices, lots of sweat, and possibly even our blood. That way, when everybody gets there, everyone has the same thing in common: We're all passionate about Jesus—passionately giving all we have for the Kingdom... faithful to the death, if necessary. We're not perfect but we're all passionate about Jesus. Communities like that know what to do: they just keep adding another leaf, and then another, and then...

ADDING A LEAF GLOBALLY

Shaye and Lisa had a passion to do church and do it right. They were in a small rural church in our county and he and I become friends. He knew about what God was doing at BNC and started asking all these questions about how to create a insurmounTABLE community. He started to make some changes, but some people don't like change. When he moved the Christian flag and the American flag from the chapel into the fellowship hall, the church's leadership had had enough of his "renegade ways" and asked him to resign.

Shaye was devastated. I asked him if we could meet. We connected at the Tall Grass Cafe where all of the pain and frustration poured out of him. In the course of our conversation I asked a very, very dangerous question: "If you could do anything right now, what would it be?" He said, "My heart beats for Russia. I served in Russia for a couple of years and my heart still beats for that place." Then, right there at the table, he started praying in Russian. He was almost fluent! I felt the power of God fall in that little restaurant. It was a total "table moment." When he lifted his head he had tears in his eyes.

I asked, "What's it going to take to make this happen?"

He said, "First we would need to find an agency to work with and get approved by them. That might take 6 months or more. Then we would need to raise funds—that usually takes 2-3 years, then…"

I said, "I think God wants you to go in August. I want to unleash a church like BNC in Russia. Let's do it."

All of our campuses caught the vision and started kicking in. $25 here, $30 there. It all added up to $66,000—enough to get things started. Four and a half months after our meeting in the Tall Grass Restaurant, BNC Russia opened in St. Petersburg. When it comes to adding a leaf, we never guessed he would go that far. I get jazzed just thinking about it—and all because of a table moment in the middle of Arkansas, and a community of believers who are committed to "adding a leaf."

UNTIL ALL ARE OFFERED A SEAT

There are a lot of cool things happening in local church communities. Globally, people are coming into the community of Christian faith at an exponential rate. Even here in America, church membership is at an all-time high. It's a battle but, by God's grace, we are definitely on the winning team. In the midst of these exciting little victories, it's invigorating to remember the bigger picture of what God is accomplishing at the table.

> The Lord is not slow in keeping his promise, as some understand slowness. Instead he is patient with you, not wanting anyone to perish, but everyone to come to repentance.—1 Peter 3:9

This is not the season to hide in fear or to relax and put our feet up and wait. These are days of great opportunity and great responsibility. Our job is to take our part the loving creative ministry that is expanding the community of believers. We are to press on until *everyone* has been offered a seat at the table.

Yes, our job is to make the invitation, and then make sure that we prepare with excellence, serving Jesus to them in our homes, in our church communities, and throughout our world. Remember though, not everyone who is invited will come. And not everyone who comes will choose to feast.

> [16] Jesus replied: "A certain man was preparing a great banquet and invited many guests. [17] At the time of the banquet he sent his servant to tell those who had been invited, 'Come, for everything is now ready.' [18] "But they all alike began to make excuses... [21] "The servant came back and reported this to his master. Then the owner of the house became angry and ordered his servant, ...'Go out to the roads and country lanes and compel them to come in, so that my house will be full. [24] I tell you, not one of those who were invited will get a taste of my banquet.'"—Luke 14:16-18, 21, 24

Listen, we don't stop until everyone has been invited. We don't stop until God says every seat at the banquet is filled. That's our job as individuals and as a community. There's a joy and there's a sense of purpose in this ministry that gives fulfillment like nothing else. This is the stuff that matters. This is the stuff that changes eternity. And this is where we *all* belong—at the table of ministry, serving and inviting and giving our lives so that all might have a chance to come to the table.

Lord Jesus,

I'm ready to get somebody at the table. I'm ready, Lord Jesus, to quit making it about me. I'm ready to make it about you. God, use me. God, thank you for church communities that makes the presentation right. God, I pray that I wouldn't sit in my I-chair and say, "Kids aren't for me," or "greeting's not for me," or "parking's not for me," or "hospitality isn't for me," or "global outreach isn't for me." God, by the power of your Spirit in me, make me willing and able to serve at the table and invite others to the table that they might feast on your goodness and bring you ultimate glory.

Amen.

AT THE TABLE WITH JESUS

Read.
- Ponder the events recorded in Acts 2.
- Make a short list of the things that made the early church insurmounTABLE

    o

    o

    o

    o

    o Imagine what it would have been like if YOU had lived as part of this community.

Pour out your heart.
- Talk honestly with Jesus about where you are right now. Share all your concerns, fears, and dreams with him.
- Would you want to live in that type of community?
- What would you need to give up in order to do so?

Listen.
- Ask the dangerous question: "Lord, if you wanted me to do anything right now, what would it be?"
- Listen carefully for his answer through the Scriptures and through his spirit speaking to your spirit.
- Commit these things to him right now, asking him to make you willing to be obedient and thanking him for providing the strength to do it.

FOR GROUP DISCUSSION

Start by sharing the most important things that you read in this chapter.

Open with a time of prayer of dependence, telling God that you are willing, as individuals and as a group, to allow him to move through you in any way he chooses.

Ponder Luke 14
- What kinds of people would you most likely invite to your church community?
- What kind of social, ethnic barriers would keep you from inviting someone into your church community?
- What barriers would keep them from coming?
- How are these things smothering the fire of your community, keeping it from being combusTABLE?

AT THE TABLE WITH YOUR TEAM

Gather with your team around a big table. Bring sheets of paper, markers, and a voice recorder.

- Read Acts 7 and 8 together. Talk about the about the selection, ministry and sacrifice of Stephen.
- Pray for God's leading and ask him how he wants to use you to "add a leaf" in your homes, in your church communities, and in the world.
- Brainstorm like crazy! Let there be no limitations on your ideas. God is able to do immeasurably be on all you ask or imagine (Ephesians). Come up with at least one idea that costs $100,000 or more. Come up with at least one idea that might require someone on your team to pay the ultimate price for expanding the community.
- Pray again, asking God to show you specifically what he would like you to do right now.

Table 3: Ministry

Leg #4: Worship

> I plead with you to give your bodies to God because of all he has done for you. Let them be a living and holy sacrifice—the kind he will find acceptable. This is truly the way to worship him.
>
> —Romans 12:1 (NLT)

detes**TABLE** [dih-tes-t*uh*-b*uh*l] adjective
1. Being or deserving to be abhorred or detested. Abominable, odious.
2. noun. Ministry Tables that have become defiled by impure motives.

The life of Jesus reflects the power of the table in ministry. Yes, Jesus saw the ministry potential in the four-legged flattopped piece of furniture and he was passionate about what happened around the table—both the good *and* bad. Time after time he used interactions around the table for eternal purposes and God's glory. He liked it when tables were used, but when he saw tables being abused; he cut loose to correct it:

> [13] When it was almost time for the Jewish Passover, Jesus went up to Jerusalem. [14] In the temple courts he found people selling cattle, sheep and doves, and others sitting at tables exchanging money. [15] So he made a whip out of cords, and drove all from the temple courts, both sheep and cattle; he scattered the coins of the money changers and overturned their tables. [16] To those who sold doves he said, "Get these out of here! Stop turning my Father's house into a market!" —John 2:13-16

> [16] …and [he]would not allow anyone to carry merchandise through the temple courts. [17] And as he taught them, he said, "Is it not written: 'My house will be called a house of prayer for all nations'? But you have made it 'a den of robbers.'"— Matthew 21:16-17

Man, that would've been something to see! Dust flying! Animals running! People yelling! …and Jesus in the middle of it all with a whip? Why would he react so strongly? The temple and the temple courts were the epicenter of the entire religious community. This was Jesus's "Father's house." This was "a house of prayer for all nations". But the temple and the table had been defiled by impure motives. The things that were happening at the table in this holy place were actually detesTABLE to Jesus… and the things that we do at the table could be the same.

Check it out. These guys were serving, they were creative, and they were at the center of the community. But their table of ministry was missing the leg of worship. The word "worship" means this: declaring his worth. Worship happens any time someone's heart recognizes the glory of God and says "God, you are worthy! By my thoughts and my actions and my words I declare your 'worth-ship'!". And let me just say this: Without the leg of worship the table *does not* stand. It *must* be there.

Excellent, God-honoring worship must be the means, and the end, of all we do.

Yes, we talked about the table of marriage, parenting, and now ministry. This is the last leg we will consider and it's critically important, it's a reminder that we need to keep everything else about the table in check in our hearts and our minds. Because "worship" isn't just something we do for 20 minutes before a sermon once a week. This is the *core* of all that we *are* and all that we *do*--it's everything.

True and proper worship is offering your body as a living sacrifice. That makes *all* of life an offering of sacrificial worship.

God, in his creativity, made us all different so we can each worship any time everywhere in different ways. Our spiritual service of worship can take off so, so many different forms:

• Worship can take place when a couple is loving, communicating, forgiving or having red-hot sex.

- Worship can take place when a parent is loving, showing honor, training, or raising their family in wisdom.
- Worship can take place in service, creativity and community.
- At church, worship can take place in the parking lot when you're waving and opening doors and parking cars.
- Worship can take place when you open up your home and share a meal.
- Worship can take place when you're dressing your kids for school, driving a car pool, turning in a report to your boss, planting the garden, or fixing a car...

Jesus once got in a discussion with a woman about the right time and place and people for worship. Jesus made on thing very clear to her: It is not where and when and who, but what's going on in the heart:

> Yet a time is coming and has now come when the true worshipers will worship the Father in the Spirit and in truth, for they are the kind of worshipers the Father seeks. God is spirit, and his worshipers must worship in the Spirit and in truth." —John 4:23-24

When and where can worship take place? Anytime, anywhere, anyone lives in a way that recognizes and reflects the glory of God and declares his worth!

This is why things got so messed up in the Temple. That place was supposed to be the house of God, a place of prayer for all nations. Yet when they lost their focus of worship, they lost everything completely. Sure, the religious machine kept working. But the heart of it was gone. The Temple was the most magnificent building ever built, and it was built for the glory of God. But when the heart of worship was lost, it was reduced to a place of commerce and greed.

When something like this happens, I smell sulfur. Worship is the target of every temptation that Satan throws our way. The ultimate goal of every strategy of Satan is to divert our hearts from worshiping God in spirit and in truth. The core of temptation (whether it's power or possessions or position) is to distract us, to cause a detour away from an intimate passionate relationship with the King of kings and the Lord of Lords. Remember when Satan took Jesus into the wilderness and tempted him? He offered him lots of really "good" stuff. He offered him food, protection, and all the possessions in the world.

[8] Jesus answered, "It is written: 'Worship the Lord your God and serve him only.'"

The evil behind what was happening at the Temple is fairly obvious:

- The moneychangers in the Temple were going for personal financial gain, as were those who were selling animals for sacrifice.
- The Pharisees and Sadducees were doing what they were doing for personal gain too-- they use their religiosity to judge and control others.
- The commoners were hoping their religious rituals would absolve them of their personal guilt.
- Beggars were hoping to capitalize on their guilt and collect a sheckle or two.

Yeah, it was a mess. It may have looked okay on the outside, but it was driven by greed and self-interest on the inside. It looked like a place of ministry, but instead it was a whole group of people sitting in their iChairs. It's the same kind of mess that makes our communities and our ministries detestable.

DISMANTLING THE detesTABLE

It would be tragic if our tables of marriage, family and ministry lost the focus of love and worship. The stakes are too high to keep playing any sort of game with our greed and self interest. This is about worship in spirit and in truth that brings glory to God and God alone. Nothing is more important. A couple of things can get us back on track.

1. Generosity shatters greed.

In Acts chapter 2, it's very clear that the early church was generous and giving. They tithed, and they gave over and above their tithe. I mean, these guys were trying to give it all away it seems. When we come into the community of God with the goal of *giving* in Jesus name rather than *receiving* from people, everything changes.

I really have to challenge church leadership on this point to. Church can so easily become a numbers game where we are counting "nickels and noses" as a way to measure our success, feel good about ourselves, to make sure that our paychecks are secure next month. That's no different than what was going on in the Temple.

Individuals and church communities need to be giving. This gets us out of the iChair so we can add a leaf and see the local and global community grow so that worship spreads and spreads.

But here's what I'm learning about tithing and giving: and when the preacher talks about it, here's the deal. You can write this down. You can Tweet it.

Givers don't kick and kickers don't give.

So if you're kicking a little bit you're telling on yourself.

> [8] "Will a mere mortal rob God? Yet you rob me. "But you ask, 'How are we robbing you?'" In tithes and offerings. [9] You are under a curse—your whole nation—because you are robbing me. [10] Bring the whole tithe into the storehouse, that there may be food in my house. Test me in this," says the LORD Almighty, "and see if I will not throw open the floodgates of heaven and pour out so much blessing that there will not be room enough to store it. Malachi 3:8-10

Giving, like everything else, can be powerful form of worship. If you do it with the right heart, you're going to be blessed. If you don't "you are under a curse." When we start giving with a heart it is intent on bringing glory to God, then God's economy starts to flow. All sorts of blessings come back *to* us and tons of people get blessed *by* us in the process. That's the way things work "at the table". The table is worth it, isn't it? Worship is worth it, isn't it?

2. Worship Trumps Works

In our culture, money is a huge stronghold, but that's not the only thing that can derail your heartfelt worship. Take a look at the words Jesus had to say to the early church in Ephesus.

> [4] Yet I hold this against you: You have forsaken the love you had at first. [5] Consider how far you have fallen! Repent and do the things you did at first. If you do not repent, I will come to you and remove your lampstand from its place. —Revelation 2:4-5

They were doing all the right stuff, but they had forgotten their first love for God. Because they had forgotten their hearts of worship, the whole table was about to be revoked. They became so focused on what *they* were doing, that they forgot who they were doing it for, and therefore could not bring glory and honor to his name through worship. In Revelation, a "lampstand" represents *ministry!* They lost the love and now they were going to lose their work. Anytime worship gets lost, ministry is in jeopardy. Another one of Jesus's friends, Martha, let works take precedent over worship:

> [38] As Jesus and his disciples were on their way, he came to a village where a woman named Martha opened her home to him. [39] She had a sister called Mary, who sat at the Lord's feet listening to what he said. [40] But Martha was distracted by all the preparations that had to be made. She came to him and asked, "Lord, don't you care that my sister has left me to do the work by myself? Tell her to help me!" [41] "Martha, Martha," the Lord answered, "you are worried and upset about many things, [42] but few things are needed—or indeed only one. Mary has chosen what is better, and it will not be taken away from her."—Luke 10:38-42

Martha was *doing* important stuff, but she wasn't doing the most important stuff. She to lost her heart of worship, lost her focus on Jesus as the head of the entire religious community that she was serving. Mary was the one who had her focus in the right place. Our heart was engaged with Jesus. It's possible that Martha could have done the same thing, even while she was going about her work. But her work was her focus, and that's why Jesus gave her such a clear correction.

In the worst cases, it's possible to become so focused on ministry that you might not even realize that you don't have a relationship with Jesus at all.

> [21] "Not everyone who says to me, 'Lord, Lord,' will enter the kingdom of heaven, but only the one who does the will of my Father who is in heaven. [22] Many will say to me on that day, 'Lord, Lord, did we not prophesy in your name and in your name drive out demons and in your name perform many miracles?' [23] Then I will tell them plainly, 'I never knew you. Away from me, you evildoers!'—Matthew 7:21-23

Listen, the most powerful temptations of Satan don't always involve sex, drugs and rock and roll, they involve ministry. He can take something that looks "good" and use it to distract us from great worship. Wow. That's brilliant.

Listen, I don't know about you, but since I started studying the tables in Scripture, I have not been able to look at any table the same way I did before. I pray it's the same for you. No longer will the table be a place in our home that gathers the junk and the leftover mail and the bill pile that we haven't gone through yet, and the tax information, and all the old pictures and the things that need to be processed and gone through. The table will be a place that Jesus considered the table to be. And that's a place where we build red-hot marriages, where we strategically nurture as parents, where we recognize loving, creative community—It's a place where we love others and minister to them, really a place where we go deep and become dear to those that we love the most.

And yet, it's possible to gain all these things and lose it all if intimate worship with Christ is not the means and the end of everything we do and everything we are.

> Come, let us sing for joy to the LORD;
>> let us shout aloud to the Rock of our salvation.
> [2] Let us come before him with thanksgiving
>> and extol him with music and song.
> [3] For the LORD is the great God,
>> the great King above all gods.
> [4] In his hand are the depths of the earth,
>> and the mountain peaks belong to him.
> [5] The sea is his, for he made it,
>> and his hands formed the dry land.
> [6] Come, let us bow down in worship,
>> let us kneel before the LORD our Maker;
> [7] for he is our God
>> and we are the people of his pasture,
>> the flock under his care.—Psalm 95:2-7

Lord Jesus,

By your mercy and grace I asked that you would give me a heart of worship, so that I might worship you in spirit and in truth, in every aspect of my life and ministry. If necessary, remove my "lampstand" of ministry so that I can know you, rest in you, and worship you like never before. I pray that this worship would overflow in my marriage, in my parenting, and in my church community. Please give me your wisdom and insight so that I can recognize the temptations of Satan that try to distract me from you with "good" things. I look to you and you alone to meet all of my core needs. To you be the honor and glory forever and ever. I will worship you and you alone.

Amen.

AT THE TABLE WITH JESUS

Ponder:
Read Psalm 139. Ask God to:
- search your heart,
- show you know your ways,
- see if there's any hurtful way in you.
- lead you in the everlasting way.

In your personal ministry, do you make a distinction between "work" and "worship"?
List specific examples of
Pour out your heart.
Meditate on Romans chapter 12:1-8.

Therefore, I urge you, brothers and sisters, in view of God's mercy, to offer your bodies as a living sacrifice, holy and pleasing to God—this is your true and proper worship.² Do not conform to the pattern of this world, but be transformed by the renewing of your mind. Then you will be able to test and approve what God's will is—his good, pleasing and perfect will.

³ For by the grace given me I say to every one of you: Do not think of yourself more highly than you ought, but rather think of yourself with sober judgment, in accordance with the faith God has distributed to each of you. ⁴ For just as each of us has one body with many members, and these members do not all have the same function, ⁵ so in Christ we, though many, form one body, and each member belongs to all the others. ⁶ We have different gifts, according to the grace given to each of us. If your gift is prophesying, then prophesy in accordance with your faith; ⁷ if it is serving, then serve; if it is teaching, then teach; ⁸ if it is to encourage, then give encouragement; if it is giving, then give generously; if it is to lead, do it diligently; if it is to show mercy, do it cheerfully.

- Take inventory of *all* aspects of your life.
- Offer each of these parts of your life as a living and holy sacrifice to him, so that everything can be your spiritual service of worship.

Listen.

- What specifically is God saying to you right now through the verses in this chapter and his Spirit?

FOR GROUP DISCUSSION

Skim over this chapter one more time.

- In your opinion, what are the most important principles presented?
- Why did you choose those over other thoughts and ideas?
- Share one thing from your own personal life that you would like to change in life of this chapter.

Consider this statement:
"The most powerful temptations of Satan don't involve sex, drugs and rock 'n roll, they involve ministry."

- Do you agree or disagree?
- Give good reasons for your opinion!
- Can you give examples of ministries that have lost their heart for worship? What did the leadership look like? What did it look like for those who follow?
- Have you ever seen a ministry lose its "lampstand" because it forgot its "first love"?

AT THE TABLE WITH YOUR TEAM

Ask God to soften your hearts, and make you willing to hear the truth from his word and from his Spirit.
Read John 2 and Matthew 21.

[13] When it was almost time for the Jewish Passover, Jesus went up to Jerusalem. [14] In the temple courts he found people selling cattle, sheep and doves, and others sitting at tables exchanging money. [15] So

he made a whip out of cords, and drove all from the temple courts, both sheep and cattle; he scattered the coins of the money changers and overturned their tables. [16] To those who sold doves he said, "Get these out of here! Stop turning my Father's house into a market!"[17] His disciples remembered that it is written: "Zeal for your house will consume me." John 2

[15] On reaching Jerusalem, Jesus entered the temple courts and began driving out those who were buying and selling there. He overturned the tables of the money changers and the benches of those selling doves, [16] and would not allow anyone to carry merchandise through the temple courts.[17] And as he taught them, he said, "Is it not written: 'My house will be called a house of prayer for all nations'? But you have made it 'a den of robbers.'" Matthew 21

- In what ways has your ministry become like the Jerusalem Temple?
- How have impure motives robbed you of the heart of worship and ministry?
- Repent as necessary, thanking him for his forgiveness.

Spend some time, as a group, pondering Psalm 95.

- In what ways could you make worship a part of *every* aspect of your ministry?
- In what ways could you, as a group, be radically generous with your tithes and offerings of money, time, talents and resources?
- Are you willing to worship and bow down to him right now at the table?

TABLE 4: A TABLE TO REMEMBER

¹⁹ And he took bread, gave thanks and broke it, and gave it to them, saying, "This is my body given for you; do this in remembrance of me."

—Luke 22:19

unforgetTABLE. [uhn-fer-get-*uh*-b*uh*l] a*djective*.
1. impossible to forget; indelibly impressed on the memory.
2. Events so important that God designed special tables so we would always remember.

I COULD NEVER forget the moment my daughter Anna was born, because, well, I don't actually remember it. Anna was my first kid and in the delivery room, I went into "beast mode", doing the turbo-young-expectant dad thing. Yeah, I had read the books and been through the classes and I was ready. But the last thing I remember was standing by Cindy while the doctors did a cesarean section on her. Then, it was lights out for me. Yup. Totally passed out. It was a special, spiritual moment as that precious new life came into the world, I'm sure. Too bad I wasn't conscious. I woke up with nurses all around me, patting wet washcloths on my head and they're like, "Congratulations, your kid's here." I said, "Oh, praise God. Now, can you stop the room from spinning?"

I do, however, remember holding her in my arms for the first time. I can see her, I can feel her, I can smell her. It's like I can live it all over again. The word "remembrance" actually means "to make alive again." That moment at the delivery table is unforgettable, just like so many,

many other moments I've had at the table—so many transforming table-moments that have rocked the course of my marriage, parenting and ministry. Throughout the writing of this book and speaking on this topic, it's like my eyes have been opened. I'll never look at a table the same again. I'll never look at life the same again. The table is where marriage, parenting and ministry [insert the rest of the subtitle!] It's good to remember things like that, to have them "indelibly impressed on the memory."

The church at Ephesus had a decent memory. They didn't forgot what they were supposed to do. When Jesus wrote to them through John in the book of Revelation, the letter was filled with A+'s and smiley faces:

> I know your deeds, your hard work and your perseverance. I know that you cannot tolerate wicked people, that you have tested those who claim to be apostles but are not, and have found them false. You have persevered and have endured hardships for my name, and have not grown weary.—Revelation 2:1-3

I don't know about you, but I pray that Christ says stuff like that about me someday. I bet the Ephesians could go through each chapter of this book, look at each leg of the three tables and say, "Cool! We passed that test!" I mean, that church was doing it right! Right? Well, yes and no.

> Yet I hold this against you: You have forsaken the love you had at first. Remember how far you have fallen! Repent and do the things you did at first. If you do not repent, I will come to you and remove your lampstand from its place.—Revelation 2:4-5

Wow. That's a major red X on the exam. Yes, if we apply the principles in this book were going to be able to experience some amazing things at the table. But before any of us start running around slapping each other on the back and throwing high-fives, we need ask a very serious question:

Have we forgotten our first love? Is he unforgetTABLE?

Christ is the beginning and the end of all that we do, and that *must not* be forgotten. He is the vine and we are the branch. Without him we can do nothing. Without his love moving through us we are nothing but noisy gongs annoying our neighbors. The key is to remember "from where we have fallen" and never stray from our "first love." It's so important that Christ instituted a time and a place to remember him and what he did for us so that we can "make it alive again."

And (you guessed it) it happens at the table.

THE TABLE TO REMEMBER

Jesus spent a lot of time with his men at the table. They celebrated life at people's tables. They watched Jesus overturn tables, they fellowship with outcasts and sinners at tables. So we shouldn't be surprised Jesus took them to the table one more time as the shadow of the cross emerged. Jesus wanted to be absolutely certain that the disciples and all believers to follow would remember what he was about to do.

> Now the Festival of Unleavened Bread, called the Passover, was approaching, [2] and the chief priests and the teachers of the law were looking for some way to get rid of Jesus, for they were afraid of the people…[7] Then came the day of Unleavened Bread on which the Passover lamb had to be sacrificed. [8] Jesus sent Peter and John, saying, "Go and make preparations for us to eat the Passover."…[14] When the hour came, Jesus and his apostles reclined at the table… [19] And he took bread, gave thanks and broke it, and gave it to them, saying, "This is my body given for you; do this in remembrance of me." [20] In the same way, after the supper he took the cup, saying, "This cup is the new covenant in my blood, which is poured out for you. —Luke 22:1-2, 7-8, 14, 19-20

This, I believe, was the *most* important "table moment" to ever take place in all of history. Nothing compares to the weight of what was going to happen at the cross, and nothing is more important than to remember it.

Just a few decades after this first "Lord's Table," the Apostle Paul, inspired by God, wrote to the church of Corinth and laid out a mandate on how to participate in and at the Lord's Table. He didn't instruct on how often or when you should go to the table, but he did give clear, specific instructions on how to prepare for this important table of remembrance:

1. Expect Differences

> [17] In the following directives I have no praise for you, for your meetings do more harm than good. [18] In the first place, I hear that when you come together as a church, there are divisions among you, and to some extent I believe it. [19] No doubt there have to be differences among you to show which of you have God's approval. —1 Corinthians 11:17-19

According to this passage, there are clearly going to be disagreements among those who come together at the Lord's table. So be it. We might wish everything in the body was completely unified during these moments, but that's just not going to be the case. Jesus lived his life perfectly, and yet Judas betrayed Jesus at the table. People that we love and serve at our tables will betray us to. I mean, these are the people that are close enough to kiss us like Jesus did.

2. Show Respect

> [20] So then, when you come together, it is not the Lord's Supper you eat, [21] for when you are eating, some of you go ahead with your own private suppers. As a result, one person remains hungry and another gets drunk. [22] Don't you have homes to eat and drink in? Or do you despise the church of God by humiliating those who have nothing? What shall I say to you?

Shall I praise you? Certainly not in this matter! —1 Corinthians 11:20-22

The early church often shared in the context of a large group meal. When you participate corporately at the Lord's Table you must come with a reverence and an understanding that the house of God is God's created institution to change the world. There may be differences between you, but you approach the Lord's Table with respect for everyone who is there and behave in a way that brings honor to all in the church.

3. Remember Why

[23] For I received from the Lord what I also passed on to you: The Lord Jesus, on the night he was betrayed, took bread, [24] and when he had given thanks, he broke it and said, "This is my body, which is for you; do this in remembrance of me." [25] In the same way, after supper he took the cup, saying, "This cup is the new covenant in my blood; do this, whenever you drink it, in remembrance of me." [26] For whenever you eat this bread and drink this cup, you proclaim the Lord's death until he comes. —1 Corinthians 11:23-26

Like any religious activity, the Lord's Table can become meaningless and repetitive. But by consciously focusing on what you are remembering, the Lord's Table can be a very meaningful place of remembrance all your life. Remembrance. here in the scripture, means, "to make alive again". You are coming to this table because of salvation. When you break that bread and drink from that cup, it's a proclamation that you recognize that Jesus body was broken and that his shed blood was the redemption for your debt to God because of sin.

4. Examine Yourself

[27] So then, whoever eats the bread or drinks the cup of the Lord in an unworthy manner will be guilty of sinning against the body and blood of the Lord. [28] Everyone ought to examine themselves before they eat of the bread and drink from the cup. [29] For those

who eat and drink without discerning the body of Christ eat and drink judgment on themselves. 1 Corinthians 11:27-29

This is serious stuff. Grace abounds and yet this passage clearly says that if you come to the Lord's Table haphazardly and you eat the bread and drink of this cup, you bring about judgment of yourself. Properly preparing for the Lord's Table is a great time to do a good heart check. You can't come to this table with bitterness in your heart. You can't come to this table with unforgiveness toward someone else. You may have things that need to be confessed to others. Or maybe you've been sitting in the iChair soaking in your own me-ology, blowing off what God's Word says about giving and serving and loving and praying.

Put yourself to the test. Let the Spirit search your heart. Check your behavior against the direction of Scripture. The Lord will lead you to any "unworthy manner" that you need to confess and correct. The Lord's Table is the place to confess all those things before God and embrace his forgiveness. That's what the cross was all about. And that's why it's vital to remember, make alive again, the cross at the Lord's Table: *Do this in remembrance that Jesus Christ died for your sins.*

In a very real way, after you have prepared properly and then go to the Lord's Table to break the bread and drink from the cup, it's just like pulling out that old picture of you holding your newborn kids as you see them crying for the first time. I remember my kids' births. As God's kid, I need to remember and keep remembering the time I became newborn because of the sacrifice that Jesus made for me. When I look at that picture and remember his sacrifice vividly—as vividly as I remember holding my newborn kids in my arms—then I can authentically love people... because he first loved me and laid his life down for me. It makes it "come alive again."

THE TABLE WORTH DYING FOR

Life is tough. It's good to remember that too. Sometimes we get the idea that if we asked Jesus into our heart everything around is just going to fall magically into place and life will be a breeze. Not at all. Jesus never promised us a rose garden, in fact he said:

> "In this world you will have tribulation, but take courage for I have overcome the world."—Matthew 16:33.

Courage is a huge part of Christian living. I think that's one of the reasons God gave us tables. Courage can be found at the table. It starts when you open that door and accept Christ's invitation to dine together in an intense personal relationship. The problem is as so many of us think we can just kick back at the table relax and sit there all comfortable. So we miss what Christ created us for—the good works that he prepared beforehand that we should walk in them. We were created to let him live through us and do amazing things. Life can feel like a marathon sometimes. But every good marathoner knows that the finish line is coming, and at the end there's a table full of icy cold Gatorade surrounded by friends and family to celebrate. When it gets tough, sometimes that vision is all that keeps the runner running.

There's a table like that waiting for us at the end of the race too—an eternal feast in the future.

> After this I heard what sounded like the roar of a great multitude in heaven shouting: "Hallelujah! Salvation and glory and power belong to our God, "Hallelujah! For our Lord God Almighty reigns... [7] Let us rejoice and be glad and give him glory! For the wedding of the Lamb has come, and his bride has made herself ready. [8] Fine linen, bright and clean, was given her to wear."(Fine linen stands for the righteous acts of God's holy people.)

> [9] Then the angel said to me, "Write this: Blessed are those who are invited to the wedding supper of the Lamb!" And he added, "These are the true words of God."

¹⁰ At this I fell at his feet to worship him. But he said to me, "Don't do that! I am a fellow servant with you and with your brothers and sisters who hold to the testimony of Jesus. Worship God! For it is the Spirit of prophecy who bears testimony to Jesus."

¹¹ I saw heaven standing open and there before me was a white horse, whose rider is called Faithful and True. With justice he judges and wages war. ¹² His eyes are like blazing fire, and on his head are many crowns. He has a name written on him that no one knows but he himself. ¹³ He is dressed in a robe dipped in blood, and his name is the Word of God. ¹⁴ The armies of heaven were following him, riding on white horses and dressed in fine linen, white and clean. ¹⁵ Coming out of his mouth is a sharp sword with which to strike down the nations. "He will rule them with an iron scepter." He treads the winepress of the fury of the wrath of God Almighty. ¹⁶ On his robe and on his thigh he has this name written:

KING OF KINGS AND LORD OF LORDS.

¹⁷ And I saw an angel standing in the sun, who cried in a loud voice to all the birds flying in midair, "Come, gather together for the great supper of God!" —Revelation 19:9-17

This is the ultimate table moment! I believe it's far beyond anything we could imagine. But it's worth trying! We read that passage again. And then again. And then read it a third time—except this time imagine that you are in the middle of it all! *Because soon enough you will be.* The rejoicing, the worshiping, the blazing entry of our Jesus, and then, the great supper of God... and *you* get a seat as an honored guest. You will be *at the table* like never before.

It's going to be a very powerful and yet humbling moment. It will be a place of honor where you will be rewarded for all the things you let Christ do through you by the power of his Spirit in you. There will be great and eternal celebration of all that he did *for* you, and all that he did *through* you as you his love touched your spouse, your children, your brothers and sisters in Christ and the lost and hurting souls of the world.

In the midst of the mess of life, the table is the place where we can connect in a vibrant way with the people that really are most important to us. Most importantly it's a place where we can connect in an intense way in a one-on-one relationship with the Father, Son, and Holy Spirit. At the table marriage, parenting and ministry *can* thrive. But will they? That's really up to you now. It's up to you to make it unforgetTABLE, to remember and "make it come alive again."

- **Remember your first love.**
- **Remember his body and blood.**
- **Remember the table that is to come.**

When we all sit round that final eternal banquet table, I pray that our stories will be vibrant and many. I pray that Christ will be glorified for all he has done and all he has done through us. Till then, I pray that our paths might cross, but if they don't cross on earth, it's inevitable, I'll see you at the heavenly table.

Shannon O'Dell

AT THE TABLE WITH JESUS

Find a table to be alone with the Lord. This is the end of the book, so maybe go back to one of the favorite tables that you have set had with him in the past weeks. Make it an extra special time with him— perhaps a fancy restaurant, or a picnic table in your favorite park. Bring some bread and a cup to drink from. You want to come to this table to remember and remember well.

Spend some time pondering Revelation 2:1-.

In what ways is your life like the Ephesians described in this passage?

In what ways are you different?

What does it feel like to you to "remember from where you have fallen."

Spend some time pondering Luke 22:1-20.

If you had been at the table with Christ and his disciples, what would you have been thinking and feeling?

What does it feel like now, to be alone with God remembering all that he did for you on the cross?

Pour your heart out to the Lord in thanksgiving. Tell him everything that you think about the cross and what he did for you.

Break the bread. Drink from the cup. Do it to remember.

AT THE TABLE WITH FAMILY AND BELIEVERS

Gather at a table with your spouse, kids and/or trusted and respected friends. Read the account of the first Lord's Table in Luke 22.

- Ask everyone about the different ways that they have remembered and celebrated the Lord's Supper throughout their lives.
- Are there any really special "table moments" that really stick out in their memory?

Read first Corinthians 11:20-27.

- Ask each person to share a little bit about what it means to them to prepare for the Lord's table by:

1. Expecting Differences
2. Showing Respect
3. Remembering Why
4. Examining Yourself

Celebrate the Lord's Table together. Feel free to be as creative or as simple as you wish.

Open a Bible to revelation 19. Pass the Bible from person-to-person, allowing each person to read a few verses in a dramatic way.

- What does everyone feel it will be like to see Christ's entrance to the banquet?
- What type of stories does each person want to be able to share and remember about how he worked through them on Earth?
- Make a short list of things that each person would like to see Christ do through them in the near future.

Close in a time of prayer, releasing these things to Christ and asking him to make it happen.

CPSIA information can be obtained
at www.ICGtesting.com
Printed in the USA
FFOW02n2056060617
36467FF

9 781512 749373